SOSIPATRA OF PERGAMUM

WOMEN IN ANTIQUITY

Series Editors: Ronnie Ancona and Sarah B. Pomeroy

This book series provides compact and accessible introductions to the life and historical times of women from the ancient world. Approaching ancient history and culture broadly, the series selects figures from the earliest of times to late antiquity.

Clodia Metelli
The Tribune's Sister
Marilyn B. Skinner

Galla Placidia
The Last Roman Empress
Hagith Sivan

Arsinoë of Egypt and Macedon
A Royal Life
Elizabeth Donnelly Carney

Berenice II and the Golden Age of Ptolemaic Egypt
Dee L. Clayman

Faustina I and II
Imperial Women of the Golden Age
Barbara M. Levick

Turia
A Roman Woman's Civil War
Josiah Osgood

Monica
An Ordinary Saint
Gillian Clark

Theodora
Actress, Empress, Saint
David Potter

Hypatia
The Life and Legend of an Ancient Philosopher
Edward Watts

Boudica
Warrior Woman of Roman Britain
Caitlin C. Gillespie

Sabina Augusta
An Imperial Journey
T. Corey Brennan

Cleopatra's Daughter
And Other Royal Women of the Augustan Era
Duane W. Roller

Perpetua
Athlete of God
Barbara K. Gold

Zenobia
Shooting Star of Palmyra
Nathanael Andrade

Eurydice and the Birth of Macedonian Power
Elizabeth Donnelly Carney

SOSIPATRA OF PERGAMUM

PHILOSOPHER AND ORACLE

Heidi Marx

UNIVERSITY PRESS

OXFORD
UNIVERSITY PRESS

Oxford University Press is a department of the University of Oxford. It furthers
the University's objective of excellence in research, scholarship, and education
by publishing worldwide. Oxford is a registered trade mark of Oxford University
Press in the UK and certain other countries.

Published in the United States of America by Oxford University Press
198 Madison Avenue, New York, NY 10016, United States of America.

Library of Congress Cataloging-in-Publication Data
Names: Marx, Heidi, author.
Title: Sosipatra of Pergamum : philosopher and oracle / Heidi Marx.
Description: New York : Oxford University Press, [2021] |
Series: Women in antiquity | Includes a new translation by
Robert Nau of the passages in the Lives of the Philosophers and
Sophists that relate to Sosipatra's story. |
Includes bibliographical references and index. |
Contents: Sosipatra as a child and student—Sosipatra as a wife, mother,
and widow—Sosipatra as teacher—Sosipatra as theurgist and oracle.
Identifiers: LCCN 2020051801 | ISBN 9780197571231 (paperback) |
ISBN 9780190618858 (hardback) | ISBN 9780197571248 (epub) |
ISBN 9780197571255 (oso) | ISBN 9780190618865 (updf)
Subjects: LCSH: Sosipatra. | Women philosophers—Turkey—Biography. |
Philosophers, Ancient—Biography. | Sophists (Greek philosophy)—Biography. |
Philosophy, Ancient.
Classification: LCC B626.S174 M39 2021 | DDC 183/.1 [B]—dc23
LC record available at https://lccn.loc.gov/2020051801

DOI: 10.1093/oso/9780190618858.001.0001

Für meine Eltern, Edda and Jerry Marx

Weil Heidilein ging nicht allein in die weite Welt hinein . . .

Contents

Acknowledgments

This book was written during a very difficult and tumultuous time in my life. I was a recent single parent, a newly appointed Associate Dean in my faculty, filling three new portfolios in three and a half years, and I was managing a complicated elder care situation in a different country and language. Writing about Sosipatra was a kind of refuge for me. Contemplating and imagining her life and the cosmos she inhabited was a source of delight and helped me to feel more myself despite the whorl of busyness I found myself immersed in. Hence, I wish to thank Nicola Denzey Lewis for suggesting this project in the first place and Stefan Vranka, my editor, for his patience and guidance along the way. I am also very grateful to Robert Nau who translated the passages from Eunapius included in the appendix of this book.

Parts of the book were presented at conferences and workshops. I wish to thank Elizabeth Depalma Digeser and Ilaria Ramelli for helping to arrange a session at the Society for Biblical Literature on late ancient biography, and Sarah Iles Johnston for inviting me to Ohio State University to participate in a workshop focused on Heidi Wendt's book, *At the Temple Gates: The Religion of Freelance Experts in the Roman Empire* where both of these wonderful scholars and other participants helped to sharpen some of my thoughts on the project.

Many chapters were written in the good company of, read by, and commented on by my outstanding writing group and band of friends, called "The Orphans": Sarah Elvins, Jennifer Dueck, Greg Smith, and Ken MacKendrick. I am very grateful for their reciprocity and encouragement.

ReMeDHe (a working group for Religion, Medicine, Disability, Health and Healing in Late Antiquity), co-founded and co-directed with my treasured friend, Kristi Upson-Saia, has been a safe haven for collaborative, engaged scholarship. And I am grateful to all of our members, and especially those who have been and are part of the board for helping to create space for interdisciplinary conversation, the mentoring of junior scholars, and the earnest co-creation of a model scholarly culture.

I have wonderful friends, many of them also colleagues, who have provided loving, generous, vital support over the past few years: many thanks to my sister Christa Marx, Blossom Stefaniw, Beth Digeser, Christine Thomas, Ellen Muehlberger, Christina Penner, Pauline Ripat, Lisa Alexandrin, Roisin Cossar, Steve Lecce, Tami Jacoby, Tracey Peter, and Greg Joyal.

Robert Shuman deserves special thanks for keeping me on an even keel, inspiring growth, advocating idleness and pleasure, and generally being a true champion of my well-being and flourishing.

Robert Chernomas has been a constant, loving presence in my life for the past few years, a source of encouragement and compassion, inspiration and a dash of intrigue. A comrade in the good fight and a companion in the pursuit of balance and harmony. Thank you!

My son, Alexander, is THE most important person in my life. He insists on it, and I am happy to oblige. He delights me endlessly with his antics and affection, his mature insight and immature goofiness. The honor of becoming his mother has made me embrace the responsibility of being an adult. My reward is that I get to be a child with him for luminous moments every day.

I dedicate this book to my parents, Edda and Jerry Marx. Thank you for everything, but especially for sending me out into the world with sufficient skills and resources to make a good life for myself and my son. It took me some time to figure out, but I think I've finally got the hang of it.

1

Introduction

This book is about a female philosopher who lived in a remarkably dynamic and exciting time in history, namely, the fourth century CE, a time when the Roman world was undergoing remarkable political, cultural (in particular religious), and even economic changes. The change that most people focus on is the slow Christianization of the Mediterranean and various kinds of responses from representatives of traditional polytheisms. We encounter our subject, Sosipatra of Pergamum, in one such response, namely, the *Lives of the Philosophers and Sophists* (*VS* for short) by Eunapius of Sardis.[1] In this work, the author traces a number of intellectual lineages in which he was himself embedded, the primary one being a lineage of ritually oriented Platonic philosophers associated with Iamblichus of Chalcis (c. 245–c. 325 CE), a third-century thinker whose own intellectual roots can be traced back to the "father of Neo-Platonism," Plotinus (c. 204–270 CE). It is in Eunapius's tracing of this lineage that we meet Sosipatra.

Ancient sources about women's lives are exceedingly rare. Outside of Christian martyrologies and hagiographies, they are even rarer. Hence, the relatively long biographical account of Sosipatra is a true exception and a real treasure for the attention it pays to this quite remarkable woman. Eunapius devotes almost as much space to her narrative as to his teacher Chrysanthius's story, whose account is the longest

---

1. I rely on the critical edition of the *Lives* by Richard Goulet: *Eunapius, Vies de philosophes et de sophistes*, Collection des universités de France. Série grecque, 508 (Paris: Les Belles Lettres, 2014). All quotations from the sections pertaining to Sosipatra (6.53–96) are from Robert Nau's translation. Quotations from other passages in the *Lives* will make use of the Loeb translation: Wilmer Cave Wright, *Philostratus and Eunapius: The Lives of the Sophists* (Cambridge, MA: Harvard University Press, 1989).

Sosipatra of Pergamum. Heidi Marx, Oxford University Press (2021). © Oxford University Press.
DOI: 10.1093/oso/9780190618858.003.0001

in the collection. But despite this relative surfeit of riches, his account of Sosipatra's life presents modern readers hoping to learn something about women's lives in Late Antiquity with a number of difficult, and in some instances intractable, challenges. Some of these are associated with the critical differences between modern biographical and historiographical standards and expectations and the conventions of ancient "non-fiction." And some of these challenges are further compounded by the fact that we have a man writing about a woman, even if in a laudatory and celebratory fashion. But these challenges are themselves pedagogically useful. They tell us something about history; they serve as an opportunity to understand past worlds and worldviews. And it is in this spirit of opportunity that this book sets out to give an account of Sosipatra's life within its sociocultural, political, and geographical context. It is a task well worth undertaking, because even if we fail, in the end, to encounter the living, breathing historical figure as she really was, we will have understood a great deal about a number of things. These include what the life of an elite woman might have been like in the fourth century CE; what opportunities she had and choices she could make on the basis of her status and gender; how male writers deployed female figures in their works to further their own intellectual agendas and projects of self-fashioning; how professional lineages were constructed and contested; and how non-Christian intellectuals sought to establish and maintain their places in the changing social and religious landscapes of Late Antiquity.[2]

My working assumption is that even if Eunapius did not give an account of Sosipatra's life that meets today's standards for "factual accuracy," he told the story of Sosipatra's life in a manner that was appealing and convincing by the biographical standards and conventions of his day, and these standards themselves are of interest to historians of the ancient past. Eunapius's biographical work can best be thought of as a form of serious entertainment for late ancient intellectuals. It is certainly concerned with "truth," but not in the sense of historical fact as we think of it. Rather it seeks to convey moral truths and ideological principles in part by presenting idealized images of intellectuals as holy men and

2. For an extensive discussion of this latter question, see Patricia Cox Miller, "Strategies of Representation in Collective Biography: Constructing the Subject as Holy," in *Greek Biography and Panegyric in Late Antiquity*, ed. Tomas Hägg and Philip Rousseau, Transformation of the Classical Heritage (Berkeley: University of California Press, 2000), 209–54.

women.[3] In other words, it is important to consider the kind of "ideological work" these narratives do. Instead of unquestioningly accepting that Sosipatra was a "powerful and spiritually gifted woman who once lived and taught in late fourth-century Pergamum," we need to be "mindful as to how Eunapius constructed her as a character within the specific genre of late antique philosophical *bioi*" (i.e., lives or biographies).[4] This book will engage with these very questions in its telling of the story of Sosipatra's life.

Sosipatra's Life in Brief

This book includes a new translation by Robert Nau of the passages in the *Lives* that relate to Sosipatra's story (see Appendix). Nonetheless, it is helpful to review some of the important events and highlights of her biography at the outset. We do not know precisely when Sosipatra was born, nor do we know when she died. It is difficult, based on the information Eunapius gives regarding her and others connected to her, to give anything like precise dates for her birth and death. Based on a number of details in his larger account, however, it seems likely that she was born in the early decades of the fourth century and may have belonged to the "final pagan generation," namely, those "pagans" who were born in the 310s and grew up and were educated during the reign of Constantine.[5] By the "final pagan generation," we mean "the last group of elite Romans, both pagan and Christian, who were born into a world in which most people believed that the pagan public religious order of the past few millennia would continue indefinitely." In other words, they were the last Romans who "simply could not imagine a Roman world

---

3. There is, at this point, a substantial secondary literature on the idea of the holy man and woman in Late Antiquity, in particular pertaining to philosophers who are presented as god-like or divinized. See for instance, Polymnia Athanassiadi, "The Divine Man of Late Hellenism: A Sociable and Popular Figure," in *Divine Men and Women in the History and Society of Late Hellenism*, ed. Maria Dzielska and Kamilla Twardowska (Krakow: Jagiellonian University Press, 2013), 13–28; Peter Brown, "The Rise and Function of the Holy Man in Late Antiquity," *Journal of Roman Studies* 61 (1971): 80–101; and Garth Fowden, "The Pagan Holy Man in Late Antique Society," *Journal of Hellenic Studies* 102 (1982): 33–59.

4. Nicola Denzey Lewis, "Living Images of the Divine: Female Theurgists in Late Antiquity," in *Daughters of Hecate: Women and Magic in the Ancient World*, ed. Dayna S. Kalleres and Kimberly B. Stratton (Oxford: Oxford University Press, 2014), 275.

5. Edward Jay Watts, *The Final Pagan Generation*, Transformation of the Classical Heritage, 53 (Oakland: University of California Press, 2015), 6.

dominated by a Christian majority."[6] This likely describes what would have been Sosipatra's outlook. However, by the time Eunapius is writing the *Lives* at the end of the fourth century, it is clear he did not participate in these earlier beliefs. It is also highly plausible, as Sosipatra outlived her three sons, all of whom reached adulthood, that she lived through the brief reign of the Emperor Julian (361–363 CE) who started life as a Christian but became an enthusiastic restorer of traditional polytheistic worship. Although it is rare to find reference to Sosipatra in standard historical accounts of this period, Julian continues to capture the imagination of non-fiction and fiction writers to this day.[7] In his novel *Julian*, Gore Vidal does have the future emperor attend dinner with Sosipatra in his youth, but Vidal presents her as a frivolous "magician" or soothsayer of sorts and not as a true philosopher.[8] Eunapius does not tell us if the two ever met, but Sosipatra was the teacher of Julian's own philosophical instructor and close advisor, Maximus of Ephesus. And as we will see, on Eunapius's account, it is Maximus who is the less substantive figure in terms of philosophical expertise and assimilation to divinity.

According to Eunapius, Sosipatra was born near Ephesus in the region of the Cayster River (the "little Meander").[9] This likely means that her family had ties to the city of Ephesus, which was one of the most important centers in late ancient Asia Minor (the west coast of modern day Turkey) (see Figure 1.1). Her family was very wealthy, and Sosipatra herself was, like most female subjects of hagiographical accounts and Greco-Roman novels, marked from childhood as especially bright, beautiful, and decorous.[10] When she was but five years old, so the story goes, two older men clothed in animal skins arrived on the estate as

6. Watts, *The Final Pagan Generation*, 6.

7. As Susanna Elm notes: "From the moment of his death, on a Persian battlefield, in 363, to today there has been hardly a year when he was not the subject of a written work in one genre or another." Susanna Elm, *Sons of Hellenism, Fathers of the Church Emperor Julian, Gregory of Nazianzus, and the Vision of Rome*, Transformation of the Classical Heritage 49 (Berkeley: University of California Press, 2012), 3.

8. Gore Vidal, *Julian*, reprint ed. (New York: Vintage, 2003), 72–77. Vidal's treatment is reminiscent of earlier scholarly assessments of many late Platonist philosophers after Plotinus, assessments that tended to be dismissive and critical of the direction his successors took in focusing on ritual. E. R. Dodds is the best exemplar of this perspective; see, for instance, E. R. Dodds, *The Greeks and the Irrational* (Berkeley: University of California Press, 1951). Subsequent work has challenged his dismissal of late Platonism as superstitious and devolved. For a discussion of scholarly attempts to rehabilitate philosophers such as Iamblichus, see Heidi Marx-Wolf, *Spiritual Taxonomies and Ritual Authority: Platonists, Priests, and Gnostics in the Third Century C.E.* (Philadelphia: University of Pennsylvania Press, 2016), 60–62.

9. Eunap., *VS* 6.54.

10. Eunap., *VS* 6.54.

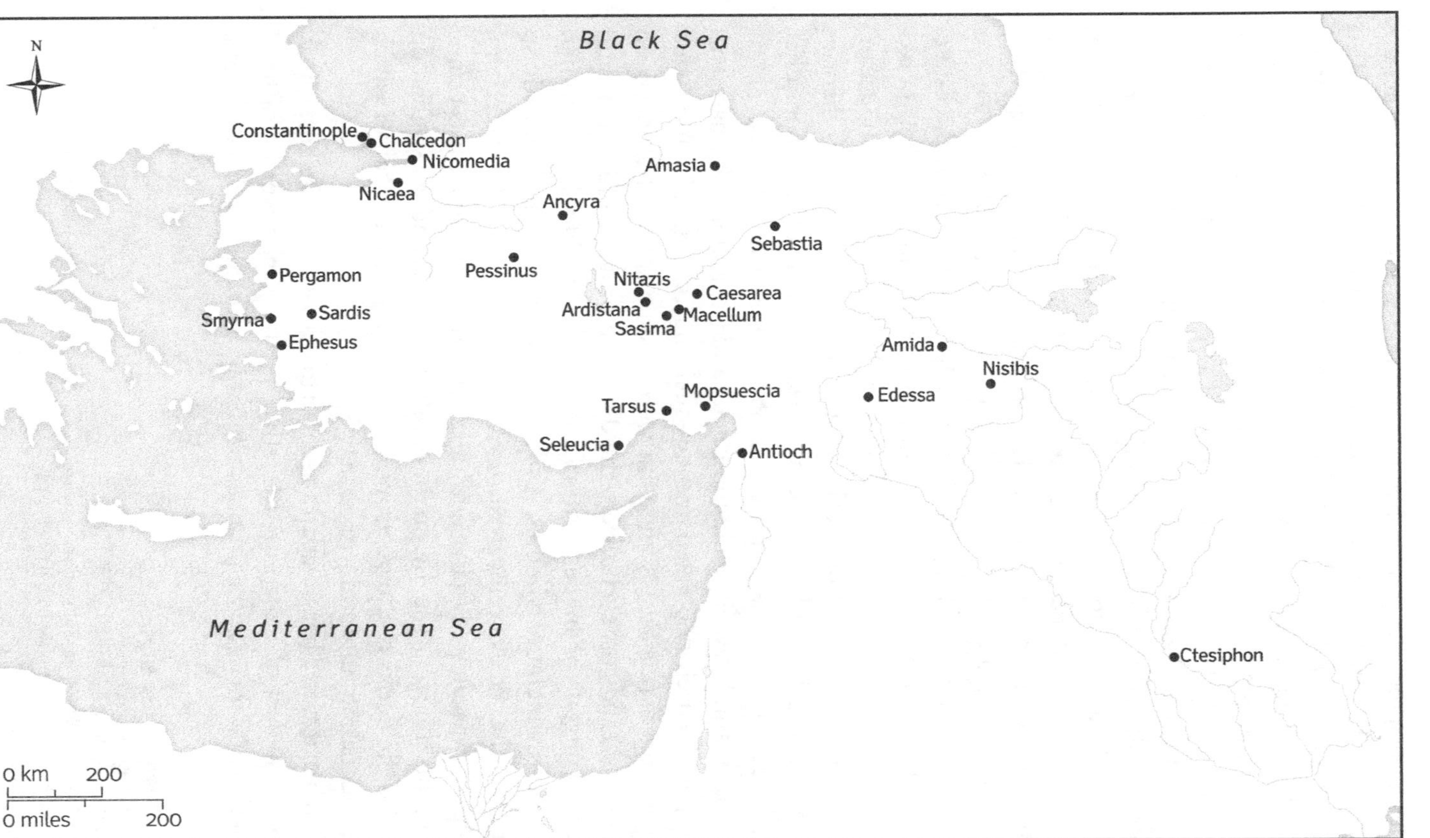

FIGURE 1.1 Map of Asia Minor in the fourth century CE.

itinerant workers. They were given a position tending vines, and at harvest time, the yield was so extraordinary that Sosipatra's father invited them to dine with him.[11] The strangers were so captivated by Sosipatra, that they made her father a deal that if he would leave her alone with them on the estate for five years, they would educate her with similarly remarkable effects. And so her father beat a hasty retreat lest he miss this opportunity to benefit his daughter by his absence.[12] When he returned after the allotted five years, the results were remarkable indeed. He was convinced she was a goddess.[13] When asked who they were, the old men reluctantly revealed that they were initiates in Chaldean lore (i.e., ancient Babylonian wisdom with a particular focus on ritual and astrology).[14] To a contemporary audience, this would have meant that they were experts in the divinization of the soul. Upon their departure from the estate, they initiated Sosipatra into their mysteries and entrusted their books to her, explaining that they would be traveling to the "Western Ocean" for a time.[15] In the cosmological understanding of late Roman theories of divinization, this indicated that they were no mere mortals but rather some sort of intermediary spirits, possibly daemons or heroes. In antiquity, the realm between the highest gods and the realm of humans was richly and densely populated by many such spirits, some of whom acted as messengers (*angeles*), some who were cosmic administrators (good *daemones*), and some who were the divinized progeny of humans and gods (demigods or heroes). All of these spirits could take on human form or inhabit human bodies. And in some accounts, they would do so as part of the cycle of reincarnation. After the departure of her teachers, Sosipatra was allowed to live her life as she saw fit on her father's estate. From this time on, "she did not have other teachers, and yet she had on her lips the books of the poets, philosophers, and orators," all of which she understood fully and with ease.[16]

When it suited her, Sosipatra decided to marry. She chose Eustathius, another subject of Eunapius's narrative, the only man worthy of her.[17] When they were wed, she prophesied that he would live five more years,

11. Eunap., *VS* 6.55–57.
12. Eunap., *VS* 6.58–61.
13. Eunap., *VS* 6.64–67.
14. Eunap., *VS* 6.67. For Eunapius's audience, this would have signaled that Sosipatra's teachers were "theurgists"—a term we will define shortly.
15. Eunap., *VS* 6.70.
16. Eunap., *VS* 6.75.
17. Eunap., *VS* 6.76.

that they would have three sons together, and that his soul, upon death, would rise as high as the orbit of the moon. She also prophesied that her own soul would rise even higher. These ideas concerning whence souls come and whither they go are part of some schools of late Platonic theology. Commentators, drawing on Platonic myths such as the fall of the soul in the *Phaedrus*, or the Myth of Er in the *Republic*, came up with theological explanations for how and why souls were embodied and how they could eventually free themselves from the constraints of this predicament. Eunapius uses Sosipatra's prophecy here to signal how superior she is even to her husband. All of this, of course, transpired as foretold.[18] Upon Eustathius's death (or possibly upon his departure, as we will discuss later), Sosipatra settled in Pergamum, where she led a school of philosophy in her home. Her friend Aedesius, Eustathius's former teacher and successor to Iamblichus's school, administered her affairs and helped to educate her sons. He had his own school in Pergamum and they shared students.[19] As mentioned earlier, one of her students was Maximus, who would eventually become the Emperor Julian's teacher in philosophy and theurgy (a form of philosophically inflected ritual practice and expertise), as well as his close advisor. Maximus helped her at one point by performing a ritual to avert a love spell cast on her by her kinsman, Philometer.[20]

In addition to teaching standard Platonic subjects—including the embodiment and ideal life of the soul and the role philosophy plays in attaining it—Sosipatra became famous for her prophetic activity, which occurred as the result of divine guidance or even possession. Eunapius refers to it as a kind of bacchic frenzy.[21] She was especially adept at what we might call "remote viewing," seeing events as they happen elsewhere.[22] This ability further convinced her students and associates that she was, in fact, some sort of divinity. Of her three sons, only one was worthy of Eunapius's attention, namely, Antoninus, who settled at the Canobic mouth of the Nile, living in a temple of Isis and devoting himself to philosophy and to the rites associated with the temple.[23] The

18. Eunap., *VS* 6.77–79.

19. Eunap., *VS* 6.80–81.

20. Eunap., *VS* 6.82–89.

21. Eunap., *VS* 6.91.

22. Denzey Lewis, "Living Images of the Divine: Female Theurgists in Late Antiquity," 277.

23. For a helpful discussion of the details of Antoninus's life included in Eunapius's *Lives*, see David Frankfurter, "The Consequences of Hellenism in Late Antique Egypt: Religious Worlds and Actors," *Archiv Für Religionsgeschichte* 2, no. 2 (2000): 186–88.

family's story ends with Antoninus's prophetic vision of the destruction of the Alexandrian temple of Serapis, which happened during the reign of Theodosius, shortly after Antoninus's death.[24]

Eunapius of Sardis and the Purpose of His *Lives*

Eunapius of Sardis was a well-educated, well-connected rhetorician who lived in Roman Lydia (a Roman province located in what is now Western Turkey) in the latter half of the fourth century. The date of his birth is a matter of some debate, but for our purposes we can fix it sometime between 345 and 349 CE.[25] He was trained in both rhetoric and philosophy. He studied rhetoric in Athens under the Christian Prohaeresius for five years from the age of fifteen through nineteen starting sometime between 361 and 364 CE, depending on his date of birth.[26] After his time in Athens, he returned home to Sardis to study philosophy under Chrysanthius, a man who had also been his grammar teacher before Eunapius left for Athens. He also seems to have received some sort of training in medicine, sufficient to be recognized by the imperial physician, Oribasius, doctor and political advisor to the Emperor Julian (361–363 CE), as an amateur expert on medicine. Oribasius spoke to Eunapius's expertise in the preface of a handbook on medicine which he dedicated to the rhetor.[27] His training in all three of these areas—rhetoric, philosophy, and medicine—accounts for the different intellectual lineages he traces in his *Lives*, the work in which Sosipatra appears. Although we have similar kinds of collective biography from earlier epochs in the form of Philostratus's *Lives of the Sophists* and Diogenes Laertius's *Lives*

24. Eunap., *VS* 6.94–96.

25. Richard Goulet discusses the problems of Eunapian chronology in volume 1 of his critical edition: Eunapius, *Vies de philosophes et de sophistes*, 5–23. He also gives an overview of what he believes is the likely chronology of Eunapius's life (24–34). This chronology draws on earlier work by the same author: Richard Goulet, "Sur la chronologie de la vie et des oeuvres d'Eunape de Sardes," *Journal of Hellenic Studies* 100 (1980): 60–72. Some of Goulet's conclusions have been challenged by other scholars. See, for instance, Thomas M. Banchich, "On Goulet's Chronology of Eunapius' Life and Works," *Journal of Hellenic Studies* 107 (1987): 164–67; Thomas M. Banchich, "The Date of Eunapius' Vitae Sophistarum," *Greek, Roman, and Byzantine Studies* 25, no. 2 (2004): 183–92.

26. Thomas M. Banchich, "Eunapius in Athens," *Phoenix* 50, no. 3/4 (1996): 304–11.

27. Philip J. Van Der Eijk, "Principles and Practices of Compilation and Abbreviation in the Medical 'Encyclopaedias' of Late Antiquity," in *Condensing Texts—Condensed Texts*, ed. Marietta Horster and Christiane Reitz (Stuttgart: Franz Steiner Verlag, 2010), 525.

of Eminent Philosophers, Eunapius's *Lives* is a strange collection at first glance and requires explanation, especially if we are to understand the place of Sosipatra in the larger narrative.

To account for the impetus for writing collective intellectual biography in Roman antiquity, we have to understand the competitive nature of rhetoric, philosophy, and medicine in this period. These biographical works were one form of collective self-fashioning and a strategy for creating group identity through the careful, deliberate, but selective "recording of relationships," both personal and textual.[28] Schools, especially of philosophy in major centers such as Athens and Alexandria, but also smaller centers such as Ephesus, Pergamum, Antioch, and Sardis, were highly competitive with each other for students.[29] And they functioned as proxy families both while students attended and after they departed to start careers. We will discuss the nature of late ancient philosophical education in much greater detail in later chapters. But suffice it to say that teachers were often thought of as parental figures and fellow students as siblings.

Eunapius's participation in three educational lineages serves as the framework for the way in which he records the genealogical connections he emphasizes in the fourth-century intellectual landscape. It is important to understand, however, that a different biographer may well have traced other connections and recorded the teaching activities of very different groups, many of which are now substantially lost to us because they were not tended to in writing by a figure such as Eunapius. Rather, their stories were likely transmitted only via oral testimony, which was the more likely form of transmission in antiquity.[30] For our purposes, it is Eunapius's participation in one of the Platonic communities of ancient Asia Minor and Lydia that is most important, a community whose lineage he works to trace back to Plotinus and his student Porphyry. It is a lineage that Eunapius most closely identifies with one of Porphyry's students in particular, namely, Iamblichus of Chalcis, who

---

28. Kendra Eshleman, *The Social World of Intellectuals in the Roman Empire: Sophists, Philosophers, and Christians*, Greek Culture in the Roman World; Variation: Greek Culture in the Roman World (Cambridge: Cambridge University Press, 2012), 149–76.

29. Edward Jay Watts, "The Student Self in Late Antiquity," in *Religion and the Self in Antiquity*, ed. David Brakke, Michale L. Satlow, and Steven Weitzman (Bloomington: Indiana University Press, 2005), 236–41.

30. Edward Jay Watts, "Orality and Communal Identity in Eunapius' *Lives of the Sophists and Philosophers*," *Byzantion* 75 (2005): 334–61.

was instrumental in introducing a ritual focus to his particular school of Platonist philosophy.

This ritually focused Platonism is most often referred to as "theurgy" or "god work." The term first appears in a work called the *Chaldean Oracles*, a work written by two legendary men named Julian, a father and son.[31] This work consists of "theological, cosmological, and theurgically practical information presented in dactylic-hexameter verse."[32] I will discuss this particular tradition of philosophy in more detail in subsequent chapters. For now, it is important to understand that after Plotinus and his emphasis on philosophy as a path for both returning to the divine source of all creation and the divinization of the soul itself by purifying it of its engagement with the material world, some of his Platonist successors began to question what role traditional rituals such as prayer, sacrifice, statue making and animating (i.e., inviting a god to inhabit his or her image), and divination and/or prophecy played in this process. Philosophers such as Porphyry and Iamblichus, despite disagreeing vehemently about animal sacrifice, believed that at least some of these rituals, all of which were associated with traditional forms of polytheistic worship, aided in these processes of purification and divinization precisely because they were divinely instituted practices.[33] In other words, they were given to humans to aid them in their efforts to maintain relationships and connections with higher beings in the cosmos and even in helping humans become more akin to these superior

31. There is a very rich literature on the *Chaldean Oracles*. Some of the most important works include Polymnia Athanassiadi, "The Chaldaean Oracles: Theology and Theurgy," in *Pagan Monotheism in Late Antiquity*, ed. Polymnia Athanassiadi and Michael Frede (Oxford: Clarendon Press, 1999), 149–84; Sarah Iles Johnston, *Hekate Soteira: A Study of Hekate's Role in the Chaldean Oracles and Related Literature*, American Classical Studies 21 (Atlanta, GA: Scholars Press, 1990); Ruth Majercik, "Chaldean Triads in Neoplatonic Exegesis: Some Reconsiderations," *Classical Quarterly* 51, no. 1 (2001): 265–96; Ruth Majercik, *The Chaldean Oracles: Text, Translation, and Commentary* (Leiden: E. J. Brill, 1989).

32. Johnston, *Hekate Soteira*, 2.

33. A number of works address the theurgical focus of Porphyry and Iamblichus as well as the debate between them over whether blood sacrifices were necessary for the salvation of the soul. See in particular Elizabeth DePalma Digeser, *A Threat to Public Piety: Christians, Platonists, and the Great Persecution* (Ithaca, NY: Cornell University Press, 2012); Aaron Johnson, *Religion and Identity in Porphyry of Tyre* (Cambridge: Cambridge University Press, 2013); Heidi Marx-Wolf, "High Priests of the Highest God: Third-Century Platonists as Ritual Experts," *Journal of Early Christian Studies* 18, no. 4 (December 22, 2010): 481–513; Heidi Marx-Wolf, *Spiritual Taxonomies and Ritual Authority: Platonists, Priests, and Gnostics in the Third Century* C.E. (Philadelphia: University of Pennsylvania Press, 2016), 13–37. The most thorough scholarly account of Iamblichus's understanding of theurgy is Gregory Shaw, *Theurgy and the Soul: The Neoplatonism of Iamblichus* (University Park: Pennsylvania State University Press, 1995).

spirits. As such, these rituals worked with the inherent connections built into the ancient cosmos by the highest god, his demiurgic creator, and all the lesser co-creative divinities, namely, gods, daemons, heroes, and so forth. Furthermore, each of these lower divinities was tasked with ordering and administering the cosmos.

At the core of this worldview was the idea of an interconnected cosmos, where levels were symbolically and ontologically linked in hierarchical ways. This worldview can be summed up in the notion of cosmic sympathy, which "is based on the idea that certain chains of noetic 'Forms' and symbols emanate from the gods through subsequent ontological grades of reality, permeating every strand of the cosmos, including the physical world."[34] In this context, a symbol is "a direct efficacious and ineffable link with divine truth, operating on the level of a talisman."[35] In other words, these symbols were built into the fabric of the cosmos from the very beginning precisely to help lower beings connect with higher ones and higher ones to assist lower ones. The theurgist, the ritually adept philosopher, was able to harness the power of these symbols and various kinds of rituals for the benefit of his or her own soul and those of others for a range of purposes, some more noble than others.[36] Eunapius's accounts of many philosophers in the Plotinian-Iamblichan lineage include vignettes that involve such ritual engagement. This is certainly the case for his narrative of Sosipatra's life. This leads us to consider where she fits in to his collective biography.

Sosipatra's Place in the Lives

It is clear that Eunapius saw Sosipatra as a crucial member of the Iamblichan lineage he was both tracing and constructing (see Figure 1.2. This is because she may have been a teacher to his beloved Chrysanthius, who was in Eunapius's mind a clear successor to the school of Iamblichus via Chrysanthius's other teacher Aedesius, one of Iamblichus's most important students. But Sosipatra had another connection to this lineage, via her husband Eustathius, who was also a student of Iamblichus but one who did not pursue a career in teaching philosophy. He chose a life

34. Crystal Addey, *Divination and Theurgy in Neoplatonism: Oracles of the Gods*, Ashgate Studies in Philosophy and Theology in Late Antiquity (Burlington, VT: Routledge, 2014), 25–26.
35. Addey, *Divination and Theurgy*, 26.
36. Addey, *Divination and Theurgy*, 26.

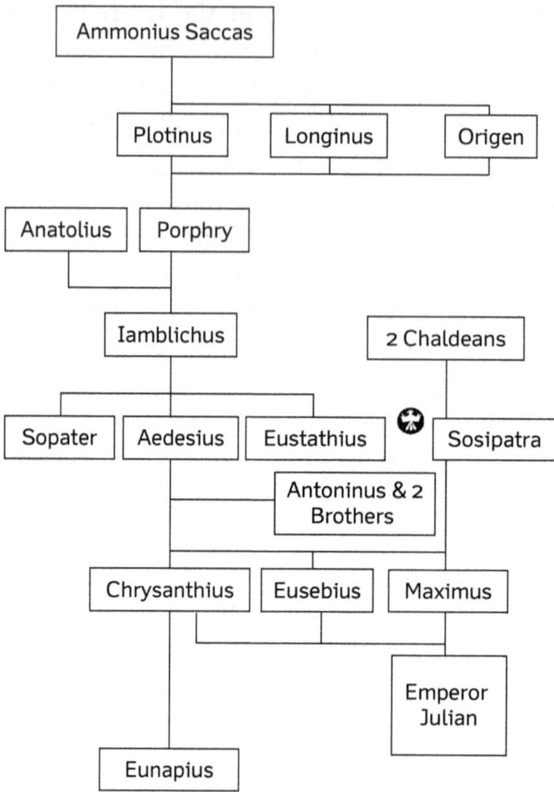

FIGURE 1.2 Succession of Philosophers, adapted from Richard Goulet, *Eunape de Sardes, Vie de philosophes et sophists*, Tome I (Paris: Les Belles Lettres, 2014), 136.

of diplomacy, politics, and civil service instead. This was a path that a number of Iamblichus's students followed.[37] To move back a generation, Iamblichus taught Sopater, Theodorus, Euphrasius, Eustathius, and Aedesius, the last of whom took over the school and taught Chrysanthius. It is also likely that he was taught by Sosipatra when she and Aedesius shared students in Pergamum after the death of her husband.

37. Both Brown and Athanassiadi make arguments that late ancient philosophers were important public figures often playing important roles at court, as ambassadors, and even at times as outspoken critics of imperial policy: Athanassiadi, "The Divine Man of Late Hellenism"; Peter Brown, "The Philosopher and Society in Late Antiquity," in *The Philosopher and Society in Late Antiquity: Protocol of the Thirty-Fourth Colloquy, 3 December 1978*, ed. Edward C. Hobbs and Wilhelm Wuellner (Berkeley, CA: Center for Hermeneutical Studies in Hellenistic and Modern Culture, 1980), 1–17.

These genealogical links are one way of thinking about how Sosipatra fits into the narrative. They explain her presence in the collective biography in the simplest and least illuminating terms. She is there because she taught Eunapius's teacher and the student of Iamblichus's successor. But the question of her place in the *Lives* is a far more complicated one when we consider that she herself does not participate in this pedagogical lineage as a student, as well as if we ask what role or roles she plays in the narrative. Eunapius seems to be making a number of points by focusing his attention on Sosipatra. In addition to situating himself and establishing his intellectual pedigree in relation to three professional domains—philosophy, rhetoric, and iatrosophistry (i.e., learned/theoretical medicine or medical education as opposed to everyday practical medicine)—Eunapius is engaged in reflecting on and constructing an ideal of intellectual life for traditional Greco-Romans in the dynamic and often hostile sociocultural and religious landscape of the late fourth century CE. This was a time when the Roman Empire was becoming increasingly Christianized, and career paths within the Christian church were attracting larger numbers of talented elite intellectuals with training similar to that of Eunapius, pulling them away from traditional vocational paths at court, in schools, and in juristic settings.

In this context, Eunapius appears to be making a number of key points with his overall narrative. He argues for a moderate form of Platonic theurgy that avoids some of the more extreme practices that could be construed as not merely harnessing but coercing cosmic forces, practices that some contemporaries would have classified as "magical." Sosipatra plays a critical role in making this point in the *Lives*. At every juncture of her story, she is open and receptive to the influence and inspiration of divinity, a mere instrument in the demiurgic project of ordering and informing the cosmos, work that is the purview of higher spirits and divine humans. At the same time, she is never seen engaging in more "aggressive" forms of ritual activity such as statue animation or casting or countering spells. As we will see, her approach to ritual and philosophical activity is most clearly juxtaposed with that of Maximus of Ephesus, who turns out to be a very ambivalent figure in the Eunapian account. Sosipatra is not the only figure Eunapius utilizes to reflect the ideal philosophical way of life, but she plays a critical role in exemplifying the kind of philosophical life that would best allow for the continued existence of Iamblichan Platonism in a Christianized world where the more problematic aspects of theurgy are downplayed or effaced in favor of an approach that maintains a clear understanding of cosmic hierarchy, despite subscribing to the idea that humans can participate in divinity in a number of ways.

The second role that Sosipatra plays in the text, I argue, is she acts as a point of critical contrast to the Christian ideal of the virginal or celibate female ascetic who is free from the taint of non-scriptural education, who does not marry or bear and raise children, and who participates in forms of self-deprivation at times so severe she compromises her health even to the point of death. Sosipatra, on the other hand, acts like a proper elite woman. She marries, bears three children, and arranges for the management of her estate through the agency of her family friend, Aedesius. There is not a whiff of the ascetic about her. In some respects, it should come as little surprise that Eunapius includes such a detailed and laudatory portrait of a holy woman such as Sosipatra, given that his Christian counterparts, that is, hagiographers, were engaged so enthusiastically in producing celebratory biographies of female martyrs and saints in large numbers—stories of women from the same class as Sosipatra roughly speaking, such as Macrina and Melania the Elder and Younger.[38] But Christians were also producing portraits of reformed prostitutes, actresses, and "nymphomaniacs" such as Mary of Egypt or Pelagia.[39] Some hagiographies also focused on cross-dressing saints such as Thecla, as well as on saints whose bodily mortifications led to the severe compromise of their physical health.[40] These include accounts of women such as Syncletica, a late ancient monastic woman who allowed her jaw bone to fester to such a degree that it was finally given a funeral while still intact, presumably as a paramedical measure

38. There is a rich literature on these female Christian figures. For an introduction to some of these figures, see Ross Shepard Kraemer and Mary Rose D'Angelo, eds., *Women and Christian Origins* (Oxford: Oxford University Press, 1999). For studies of individual figures, see, for instance, Elizabeth Clark, *The Life of Melania the Younger: Introduction, Translation, and Commentary* (New York: Edwin Mellon Press, 1984); see also Elizabeth Clark's forthcoming book in this series on Macrina.

39. For further reading on "holy harlots" as they are sometimes called, see Virginia Burrus, *the Sex Lives of the Saints: An Erotics of Ancient Hagiography* (Philadelphia: University of Pennsylvania Press, 2004); Patricia Cox Miller, "Is there a Harlot in This Text? Hagiography and the Grotesque," *Journal of Medieval and Early Modern Studies* 33, no. 3 (2003): 419–35; Benedicta Ward, *Harlots of the Desert: A Study of Repentance in Early Monastic Sources* (Kalamazoo: Cistercian Publications, 1978).

40. For an introduction to the figure of Thecla, see Jeremy W. Barrier, *The Acts of Paul and Thecla: A Critical Introduction and Commentary* (Tübingen: Mohr Siebeck, 2009). For a study of her popularity in Late Antiquity see, Stephen J. Davis, *The Cult of St. Thecla: A Tradition of Women's Piety in Late Antiquity* (Oxford: Oxford University Press, 2001). For cross-dressing saints, see Kristi Upson-Saia, "Gender and Narrative Performance in Early Christian Cross-Dressing Saints' Lives," *Studia Patristica* 45 (2010): 43–48.

to stop the spread of necrosis.[41] Eunapius presents a counter-portrait in his biographical sketch of Sosipatra to what would have seemed like extreme and disruptive experiments in gender construction for many traditional Greco-Roman polytheists.

My approach to the question of what roles Eunapius asks Sosipatra to play in his narrative draws on insights from a number of feminist historiographers such as Judith Butler, Elizabeth Clark, Amy Richlin, and Joan Scott.[42] In addition to presenting what I hope will be a rich contextualization of the rather sparse details Eunapius offers us about his heroine such that readers will learn something about the life of elite intellectual women in the late fourth century CE Roman East, I also advance the argument that Sosipatra frequently "vanishes" from the text as a real historical woman and is replaced by these two "Sosipatra functions," to use Clark's term, namely, her function as a critic of both overly zealous theurgists and overly enthusiastic Christian female ascetics.[43] The exploration of these "Sosipatra functions" will happen primarily in the final chapter of the book in the context of a discussion of our subject as an oracle, diviner, and theurge. The other chapters trace her story chronologically from childhood through to the time when, as a widow or as a separated woman, she led her own philosophy school in Pergamum.

---

41. Pseudo-Athanasius, *Vita Syncletica* 111 (PG 28, 1556).

42. Judith Butler, *Gender Trouble: Feminism and the Subversion of Identity*, Thinking Gender (New York: Routledge, 1990); Elizabeth A. Clark, "The Lady Vanishes: Dilemmas of a Feminist Historian after the 'Linguistic Turn,'" *Church History* 67, no. 1 (1998): 1–31; Amy Richlin, *Arguments with Silence: Writing History of Roman Women* (Ann Arbor: University of Michigan Press, 2014); Joan W. Scott, "Gender: A Useful Category of Historical Analysis," *American Historical Review* 91, no. 5 (1986): 1053–75.

43. Clark, "The Lady Vanishes," 28.

2

Sosipatra as a Child and Student

We can start this chapter on Sosipatra's childhood with an ancient image—a young girl holding a dove or a pair of doves, a depiction found on many funerary steles in the Greco-Roman world (Figure 2.1). It is an idealized portrait of girlhood, namely, the picture of a girl at play with her favorite pets—an image that evokes the happiness of childhood. But it also evokes loss, not just the loss of the child herself but also of the life she was to have, a life of marriage, childbirth, and childrearing; a life symbolized by the doves she holds, symbols of marital concord and fidelity.[1] Eunapius's description of Sosipatra's childhood and education, though it departs in significant ways from certain female norms of the time, is akin to the funerary portrait in its idealization of its subject. This is evident, for instance, if we compare it with the autobiographical, but no less rhetorical, portrait Augustine paints of his own childhood a few decades later, a childhood where strict parenting and harsh discipline in the context of his schooling were experienced as forms of necessary tyranny, necessary because of his own less than ideal behavior and lack of virtue on many occasions. Augustine embeds his own microcosmic experiences and choices in a macrocosmic drama parsed into moments that include primordial creation, fall, redemption, and return. His account of his own moral and intellectual development feels more familiar to modern readers than Eunapius's stable descriptions of his subjects, because modern biography focuses on personal development and change over time. Sosipatra's biography is far more static, and in this respect, it more closely resembles the conventions of biographical

---

1. Keith Bradley, "Images of Childhood in Classical Antiquity," in *The Routledge History of Childhood in the Western World*, ed. Paula S. Fass (London: Routledge, 2013), 26.

Sosipatra of Pergamum. Heidi Marx, Oxford University Press (2021). © Oxford University Press.
DOI: 10.1093/oso/9780190618858.003.0002

FIGURE 2.1 Marble grave stele of a little girl ca. 450–440 BCE, Greek. Metropolitan Museum of Art, New York City. Public domain, https://www. metmuseum.org/art/collection/search/252890.

and hagiographical writing of the ancient world, including the Gospel accounts of Jesus. According to these conventions, individuals are born with a certain rather fixed character, and life presents opportunities for this character to be revealed rather than to develop and change. As Eunapius makes clear, Sosipatra's character was marked as extraordinary from very early in her life. Despite the way in which his telling of her life reflects these biographical conventions, her story is also embedded in and informed by a cosmology no less complex than Augustine's, namely, a late Platonist one, a cosmology that we will explore further as her individual story unfolds.

Sosipatra's Early Life in Context

According to Eunapius, Sosipatra was born in the Roman province of Asia, near the city of Ephesus, to a wealthy family. He first refers to her as an infant or small child, which means she was a child younger than five years old, by far the most precarious time of life for children in antiquity.[2] Knowing where she came from and her social standing in early life tells us quite a lot. Ephesus was the capital of the province of Asia at the time. It had been granted this imperial favor in 29 BCE, but its inhabitants, especially its elite citizens, frequently found themselves in a dynamic competition with other cities in the region, in particular with Sosipatra's future home Pergamum, for the continuation of this honor.[3] The city of Ephesus was closely associated with one of the seven wonders of the ancient world, namely, the extra-urban temple of Artemis (see Figure 2.2). And although the city experienced misfortune in the third century as a result of earthquakes and Gothic invasions, by Sosipatra's time it had achieved stability and restored many important public and religious buildings.[4]

In the fourth century, it underwent a slow transformation into a more Christian city, but this would have been difficult to detect in the first half of the century when Sosipatra was growing up in the vicinity. In reality, the city would have functioned in terms of its public institutions, religious calendar, and everyday affairs in a manner quite continuous with its past. However, before we can consider how the very young Sosipatra might have experienced this environment, we have to discuss the demographic realities she faced in early childhood. In other

2. Eunap., *VS* 6.54.

3. Peter Sherrer, "The City of Ephesos from the Roman Period to Late Antiquity," in *Ephesos: Metropolis of Asia*, ed. Helmut Koester (Cambridge, MA: Harvard University Press, 1995), 4. For a discussion of elite participation in the competition between cities for imperial honors, see Athanasios Rizakis, "Urban Elites in the Roman East: Enhancing Regional Positions and Social Superiority," in *A Companion to Roman Religion*, ed. Jörg Rüpke (Malden, MA: Blackwell, 2007), 317–30.

4. Sherrer, "The City of Ephesos," 15–25.

FIGURE 2.2 Current site of the Temple of Artemis at Ephesus. Courtesy of the author. Photo by author.

words, she had to survive childbirth and the first years of life, a feat that was, statistically speaking, no small challenge.

Life expectancy at the time of birth was about twenty-five years in the ancient Mediterranean.[5] The first year of life was most precarious, and some historical demographers maintain that about 50 percent of all children died by the age of ten.[6] Weaning was a particularly dangerous time, as it exposed children "to an increasing number of bacteria and parasitic infections" which could result in "fatal diarrhoeal disease and malnutrition."[7] Sosipatra's chances of survival may have been slightly better than children of less advantaged households, but not by much. The most common illnesses that led to child mortality would likely have been conditions such as malaria, typhoid, and tuberculosis.[8] Other

5. Bradley, "Images of Childhood," 28.
6. Bradley, "Images of Childhood," 28.
7. Mary E. Lewis, *The Bioarchaeology of Children: Perspectives from Biological and Forensic Anthropology* (Cambridge: Cambridge University Press, 2007), 100.
8. Bradley, "Images of Childhood," 30. Most of these diseases do not show up clearly in the osteological record and are therefore hard to verify. However, it is not a stretch to draw parallels between the causes of childhood mortality in antiquity and those in periods with more reliable recording practices.

diseases threatening but not always fatal to small children were anemia, rickets, and scurvy.[9] Despite high infant mortality rates, children were cherished and valued. They were not considered marginal beings in ancient society. Romans certainly practiced abortion, infanticide, and exposure on occasion, usually under conditions of extreme poverty. But overall there is overwhelming evidence that children were of central societal importance and deeply mourned when they met an early death.[10]

Ancient childhood as a distinguishable phase of life was generally divided into three stages: infancy (from ages one to five), girlhood/boyhood (ages six to eleven or twelve), and adolescence (ages twelve to seventeen or eighteen). Boys were shaped and molded for civic society, girls for marriage and motherhood.[11] We meet Sosipatra at the end of the first stage of childhood when she is five years old.

It is clear from Eunapius's account that Sosipatra came from a family of considerable wealth and elite social standing. When he states that she came from the region of the Cayster River near Ephesus and that her father owned country estates, we can reasonably assume that he had a home in the city and multiple estates devoted to various forms of agricultural activity, certainly viniculture at one of them, which would have served as sources of revenue for his family. It is impossible to tell from Eunapius's descriptions just how wealthy her father was in terms of his properties. We know that some wealthy individuals during this period were able to amass immense landholdings. For instance, based on the *Life of Melania the Younger* we know that "senatorial families might have property in more than six provinces of the Roman Empire," and their annual incomes might be the equivalent of a "living for about twenty-four thousand families a year."[12] Olympias, the friend and benefactor of John Chrysostom, one time bishop of Constantinople in the late fourth century CE, had property in four provinces and possessions in the eastern capital. The latter included "three houses, baths, a mill, and various suburban properties." She donated these to the church "along with

9. Mary E. Lewis, "Diseases and Trauma in the Children from Roman Britain," in *Oxford Handbook of the Archaeology of Childhood*, ed. Sally Crawford, Dawn M. Hadley, and Gillian Shepherd (Oxford: Oxford University Press, 2018), 471–72.

10. Christian Laes, *Children in the Roman Empire: Outsiders Within* (Cambridge: Cambridge University Press, 2011), 8, 99. Maureen Carroll, "Archaeological and Epigraphic Evidence for Infancy in the Roman World," in *Oxford Handbook of the Archaeology of Childhood* (Oxford: Oxford University Press, 2018), 149.

11. Bradley, "Images of Childhood," 18–19.

12. Elizabeth A. Clark, "The Lady Vanishes: Dilemmas of a Feminist Historian after the 'Linguistic Turn,'" *Church History* 67, no. 1 (1998): 18.

FIGURE 2.3 Interior of the Terrace Houses at Ephesus. Courtesy of the author. Photo by author.

the equivalent of $900 million."[13] This kind of wealth easily translated into social, political, and cultural influence in Late Antiquity, and, when it became concentrated in the hands of young to middle-aged widows, could cause considerable familial consternation.

Even without knowing precisely her father's degree of affluence, it is safe to say that Sosipatra would have enjoyed a great deal of comfort and privilege compared with the vast majority of late ancient children. We can get a sense of the kind of amenities she would have enjoyed when we consider architectural examples of the late ancient domus (an urban home) and villa (a rural estate). We might even consider as a possible example of her urban home the terrace houses in late ancient Ephesus, which have been excavated and which exhibit a grandeur, beauty, and level of comfort that does not fail to impress visitors today even in their ruined state (Figure 2.3). Her family's homes would certainly have been beautifully decorated, perhaps with glass or tile mosaics, frescoes, and statuary. They would have been well appointed and spacious by contemporary standards, with multiple spaces for dining, playing, entertaining, and even bathing.

13. Clark, "The Lady Vanishes," 18.

FIGURE 2.4 Silver plate from Ephesus, relief of Diana of the Hunt riding a stag, fourth century CE. Staatliche Museen zu Berlin. Courtesy of the author. Photo by author.

Sosipatra and her family could have escaped from the city and its heat, noise, pollution, and "contagion," to their rural residences where, in the Late Antique period, provincial elites tended to spend more time managing their estates. Her family's homes would likely have had libraries, rooms like the one in the Ephesus terrace houses, decorated with frescoes or statues of the Muses, of philosophers, comic and tragic writers, and/or the masks of tragedy and comedy.

Comfort and luxury would have also been enhanced through household and personal textiles, which, given their ephemeral nature, tend not to survive but are frequently alluded to in texts of various genres, including moralistic ones that criticize extravagance in dressing and outfitting the home, especially bedrooms.[14] Other luxury objects that would have been present in wealthy households included items such as silver vessels, jewelry, fine ceramics, and so forth (Figure 2.4). Decoration in the house would have celebrated and promoted a sense of

14. Henry Maguire, "The Good Life," in *Late Antiquity: A Guide to the Postclassical World*, ed. G. W. Bowersock, Peter Brown, and Oleg Grabar (Cambridge, MA: Belknap Press of Harvard University Press, 1999), 238–39.

abundance by representing images "drawn from nature" and depictions of divinities associated with feasting, drinking, and fecundity.[15]

Many of the household objects associated with projecting luxury and abundance that would have surrounded Sosipatra as a child would have also had a religious dimension as most of them would have borne religious imagery of one kind or another. Studies of elite household interiors, furnishings, and daily use objects from Pompei make the ubiquity of this kind of imagery—namely, depictions of divinities and mythological scenes—abundantly clear for an earlier epoch in the Roman West. But there is no reason to doubt that the same would not also hold for a late ancient "pagan" household in the eastern Empire.[16]

Both urban and rural residences in the post-Constantinian period were sites of fierce competition among late Roman elites; they served as "an argument for social belonging."[17] This architectural impulse is mirrored, as we noted, in the introduction in Eunapius's creation of an illustrious intellectual lineage for himself and the subjects of his biography. In general, Sosipatra's father would have likely participated to some degree in this architectural competition. And as a consequence, Sosipatra, by virtue of her status, would have experienced life as pleasant and comfortable whether in the city or the country.

Discussion of late ancient residences leads us to consideration of the structures of the ancient elite household. In addition to the comforts of a well-appointed home, Sosipatra would have been born into the rich and complex social landscape of an elite household. This would have included her closest family members, not just parents and siblings, but also often grandparents, and even maternal aunts and uncles.[18] It could have also included nurses, teachers and tutors, household managers, gatekeepers, kitchen staff, tenants, eunuchs, and a wider array of other servants of varying status, both free and slave.[19] Among all of these household members, especially those who were servants and tenants, we could expect a wide diversity of social backgrounds, levels

15. Maguire, "The Good Life," 246–47.

16. Annemarie Kaufmann-Heinimann, "Religion in the House," in *A Companion to Roman Religion*, ed. Jörg Rüpke (Malden, MA: Blackwell, 2011), 188–201.

17. Kimberly Diane Bowes, *Houses and Society in the Later Roman Empire*, Duckworth Debates in Archaeology (London: Duckworth, 2010), 94–95.

18. Ville Vuolanto, "Elite Children, Socialization, and Agency in the Late Roman World," in *The Oxford Handbook of Childhood and Education in the Classical World*, ed. Judith Evans Grubbs and Tim Parkin (Oxford: Oxford University Press, 2013), 588.

19. Vuolanto, "Elite Children" 588.

of education, and responsibilities. In general, elite children were "born into a household community where servile dependents, female nurses, and male chaperones (pedagogues)" carried out the everyday tasks of childrearing and provided "instruction in the first years."[20]

If her mother survived the dangers of childbirth (her mother is never mentioned), Sosipatra may have been nursed by her, but she is likely to have had a wet nurse as well. This woman would have been carefully chosen on the basis of her character and ability to inculcate proper virtue, manners, and speech in her charge. Although Eunapius's description of Sosipatra implies she was by nature a child of extraordinary character and birth, most elite children would have undergone processes of socialization that would have aimed at molding them into this ideal. Nurses and possibly physicians would have massaged Sosipatra's body to attain an ideal shape and would have swaddled it when she was very young in order to do the same.[21] Children were generally seen as passive and malleable, lacking in critical agency, and in need of formative, educative intervention.[22] This process would likely have started very early for a child such as Sosipatra.

Before we turn to evidence in the text itself that this process was well under way in Sosipatra's case by the time she was five, we should also consider that as she was a child, play was likely an important part of Sosipatra's daily life, whether with other children or alone with toys and pets or with nurses and caregivers. She may have had opportunity to play with other children of her social class, but it is more likely that her playmates were other children in her household, those of servants and slaves. From images and artifacts, we know that children played with a wide variety of toys such as rattles, dolls (those representing both humans and animals), pull toys such as chariots, hoops, dice, board games, knuckle bones, and balls (Figure 2.5). Sosipatra may also have had a set of letters carved into blocks or made out of ivory.[23] She could have had pets with which she played. Doves, dogs, cats, geese, and roosters all appear on funerary stele for children. These animals were also thought of as teachers of virtues, along with well-spoken nurses and pedagogues.[24]

20. Bradley, "Images of Childhood," 19.
21. Bradley, "Images of Childhood," 21.
22. Bradley, "Images of Childhood," 18.
23. Bradley, "Images of Childhood," 25–26. See also Carroll, "Archaeological and Epigraphic Evidence," 150.
24. Bradley, "Images of Childhood," 26.

FIGURE 2.5 Marble relief of children playing, fifth century CE. Constantinople, Staatliche Museen zu Berlin. Courtesy of the author. Photo by author.

Sosipatra's early induction into family and society would also have had a religious dimension. She would have been welcomed into the world and into her family through a series of rituals that would have reflected local traditions and local divinities. We know quite a lot about these ceremonies for classical Athens, for instance, and less so for late ancient Asia Minor. But she would have been bathed, presented to her parents, ritually named after eight days of life, and adorned with a *bulla*, a protective amulet worn around the neck as a locket.[25] As she grew up, she would have participated in one way or another in household and civic rituals and celebrations on a daily, monthly, and annual basis. From making offerings on the household shrine or hearth and at mealtimes, to participating in city wide processions and festivals, Sosipatra's life would have been rich in ritual occasions. Encounters and interactions with representations of gods and goddesses would have been frequent and unavoidable in Sosipatra's world, a world which was still "full of gods" in the early fourth century. In terms of her larger environment, especially in an urban setting such as Ephesus, Sosipatra would have been surrounded by sacred places: "temples, statues, and festivals were so omnipresent that they mostly faded into the sensory background as a

25. Bradley, "Images of Childhood," 27.

sort of white noise or ambient odor that lurked without much acknowl-edgment within the empire's physical space."[26] Given that Sosipatra grew up near Ephesus and possibly spent time in the city, she would have been exposed to a this sort of religious environment. We might even imagine her, as a young elite girl, participating in the processions of the goddess Artemis (Diana) (Figure 2.6), processions that started and fin-ished at the great suburban temple and wound their way along a sacred way through the city. Young girls, as depicted in Xenophon's *Ephesian Tales*, would weave and carry a new garment (*peplos*) for the goddess in some of these processions. And it was during these festivals that young men and women would be on display for each other as potential mar-riage partners.

Even if Sosipatra spent most of her time on her father's rural estates, she would have been surrounded by a wide variety of sacred sites such as "large temple complexes, grottoes and other rustic sacred locations . . ."[27] Families even supported private temples on their villas along with their priesthoods.[28]

Sosipatra's Education

To turn to Sosipatra and her story directly, we catch our first glimpse of her in Eunapius's narrative when she is five years old. He begins his story by immediately telling the tale of her unique education. One day, he tells us, two men arrived at her father's estate looking for employ-ment. They were older, one more so than the other, and they carried full wallets or satchels and wore animal skins on their backs.[29] They asked to work tending the newly sprouting vines, which means they must have arrived in the springtime, and they were granted their wish. Already the reader's curiosity is piqued. What kind of men were they? They were itinerant workers but appeared to have wealth of some sort (as it

26. Edward Jay Watts, *The Final Pagan Generation*, Transformation of the Classical Heritage, 53 (Oakland: University of California Press, 2015), 17–18. Watts uses Alexandria to illustrate his point, where there were "almost 2,500 temples in the city, nearly one for every twenty houses" (18).

27. Watts, *The Final Pagan Generation* 19.

28. Watts, *The Final Pagan Generation* 22. Watts notes that the "temples could also serve as the center for the family's funerary cult and the rituals associated with it" (22).

29. Eunap., *VS* 6.55. Eunapius's description of these figures' attire would likely have been signifi-cant to a late ancient reader. But it is difficult to trace today what cultural or ethnic connotations he may have been conjuring with this reference to "animal skins."

FIGURE 2.6 Statue of Artemis of Ephesus, Ephesus Museum. Courtesy of the author. Photo by author.

turns out their wallets were stuffed with books and not money, but that is no less strange). And their clothing was also unusual. They weren't dressed as philosophers or typical laborers. Under their care, the vines flourished and produced an incredible harvest "beyond expectation."[30] This fact came to the attention of the estate owner, Sosipatra's father, who happened to be on site with his daughter. There was general speculation that this outcome was the result of some divine intervention.[31] In thanks for their stewardship, Sosipatra's father invited the two vine keepers to dinner and treated them to "Greek hospitality."[32] Sosipatra was at dinner as well, and they were "stung deeply and conquered by the beauty and forwardness of the little child."[33] They offered to repay her father for his hospitality by repeating their vine-tending success with Sosipatra in the form of educating her. The results, they promised, would be "a gift that reaches the heavens and extends to the stars."[34] They also claimed to be her parents in a truer sense than her father. All her father had to do, in order to benefit from their offer, was to depart from his estate for five years and leave Sosipatra in their care. They told him that if he did this, no harm would come to her in that time, including no sickness or death. Furthermore, his wealth would "burgeon and sprout anew spontaneously from the land," and his daughter would become something greater than an ordinary woman.[35] Sosipatra's father handed her over to the men's care, instructing his estate manager to furnish them with anything they might need, and he "set out as if running away from his daughter and the estate too."[36] The two men, "whether they were heroes, or spirits, or a race in some way more divine," cared for Sosipatra for the appointed time, "and not one person knew into what mysteries they inducted her and it was obscure even to those who really wanted to know what purpose they had in mind for making her divine."[37]

30. Eunap., *VS* 6.56.
31. Eunap., *VS* 6.56.
32. Eunap., *VS* 6.58.
33. Eunap., *VS* 6.58.
34. Eunap., *VS* 6.59.
35. Eunap., *VS* 6.60. Ilinca Tanaseanu-Döbler notes that this "motif has some reminiscences of the encounter of Demeter and Metaneira" in the *Homeric Hymn to Demeter*, 212–64. Ilinca Tanaseanu-Döbler, "Sosipatra—Role Models for Pagan 'Divine' Women in Late Antiquity," in *Divine Men and Women in the History and Society of Late Hellenism*, ed. Maria Dzielska and Kamilla Twardowska (Krakow: Jagiellonian University Press, 2013), 130.
36. Eunap., *VS* 6.61–62.
37. Eunap., *VS* 6.63.

Eunapius gives us quite a lot of helpful information in the foregoing description of Sosipatra's family of origin, their social status, along with details about her childhood and education. It is an idealized portrait, hence, there is little in it that can be relied upon as "fact." But it points us in many interesting directions for contextualization.

Sosipatra's education, as described by Eunapius, is unique to say the least, and we will need to discuss how to approach its more mythical features in historiographical terms, something which we began to do in the introduction to this book. Regardless of these features, Sosipatra's education would have already begun by the time she was five, either from a nurse who taught her letters or a dedicated teacher. The Christian writer Jerome advised a recipient of one of his letters to encourage young girls to learn by giving them letters carved out of ivory or boxwood to play with.[38] Sosipatra's mother or another female household member may have already begun to teach Sosipatra how to spin and weave, skills most girls learned regardless of social class. And she would have also begun to learn manners in company and at the table. Indeed, Eunapius refers to her father's style of hospitality as "Greek." This implies that he was a culturally superior man in his mode of living and entertaining, "Greek" (Hellene) often being contrasted with barbarian or other more specific ethnic identities. The fact that the mysterious vine tenders who became Sosipatra's teachers were so impressed with this form of hospitality and so charmed by her comportment implies that she had already been trained sufficiently in this culture and manners to be present at the table with her family and guests.

We catch a glimpse of these table manners in a work by the Christian author Clement of Alexandria in his aptly entitled *Paedagogus*. This term is sometimes translated as "teacher" but a *paedagogus* was just as likely to have been the attendant, often a slave, who chaperoned young boys to school and back ensuring their safety and also their decorum.[39] The work by Clement is devoted to inculcating "Christian morals" in his diverse urban population of believers, especially as they pertained to moments when this motley crew shared a communal meal. The moral guidelines he records reflect a very elite understanding of decorum and manners, more than they reflect a distinctly Christian ethic. They are,

38. Jerome, *Letter 107*, "To Laeta."

39. Keith Bradley, *Discovering the Roman Family: Studies in Roman Social History* (New York: Oxford University Press, 1991), 37–64, 71–72. See also Watts, *The Final Pagan Generation*, 30.

for the most part, the table manners of elite Greco-Romans who have imbibed deeply of Stoic ethics. This early Christian text is helpful for imagining the kind of behavior that would been expected and exhibited at the table of Sosipatra's father. We can imagine that Sosipatra, her father, and their guests all recognized in each other's comportment at dinner a common behavioral koine.

We find a helpful summary of Clement's injunctions about table manners in the following passage:

> Hands and chins were to be kept clean, so too for the couches on which diners reclined. Small amounts of food only were to be taken from the serving tables, at appropriate moments, and they were to be eaten slowly. There were to be no facial contortions while swallowing, no talking while eating, no eating and drinking at the same time, no gulping, spitting, or coughing; the head was not to be turned, the eyes were not to roll, and the nose was not to be blown while drinking. Belching and sneezing, if unavoidable, were to be quietly suppressed and so on.[40]

This description of elite table manners speaks to the context in which Sosipatra met her future teachers while she was visiting one of her father's estates at the time of the grape harvest. When Eunapius describes how impressed they were with her beauty and charm, he may have had in mind, as part of his image of her, her decorous behavior at dinner as a sign of her early formation by her parents and other members of her father's well-ordered, well-managed household. Another part of his image is certainly her innate intellectual and spiritual aptitude.

What are we to make, however, of the story Eunapius tells us of the way in which teachers were employed for the five-year-old girl and the manner of her education? Let us review the story briefly. Two itinerant workers wandered onto her father's estate to tend vines and assist in the harvest. This was not unusual in Late Antiquity. Indeed, using itinerant labor was a common practice in certain agricultural sectors and at certain times of the year. But these workers would have generally been poor and uneducated. The two workers in question here were neither. They carried "ample wallets," and they were knowledgeable about everything from agriculture and estate management to the philosophy of Plato and

---

40. Bradley, "Images of Childhood," 27.

the poetry of Homer. And the story becomes even more unlikely and fantastic from this point on.

The men claimed that if Sosipatra's father was impressed with their management of his grape harvest, he would be even more impressed with their cultivation of his daughter's mind and soul. The basis for their claim was their superhuman abilities which were only partially evidenced by their management of his vines, but which would be fully apparent in their education of Sosipatra. They also guaranteed her protection, her life itself; she would be free from disease, harm, and death for five years. Given the fact that on average 50 percent of all children in Greco-Roman antiquity died before the age of ten, this promise alone would have provided Sosipatra's father with strong reasons to leave her in the older men's care.

It was not unusual for children to be given over to teachers, even in these instructors' home schools, for periods of time. But this generally happened in later stages of their education and infrequently in the case of girls. But trying to make sense of the story of Sosipatra's education in terms of contemporary pedagogical practices may be a vexed approach if it is the only approach one takes. It is important to contextualize her story using information we have about the education of girls in Late Antiquity. But we also have to consider what Eunapius is doing with this story and the various assumptions about both intellectual development and cosmic order he would have shared with his readers, assumptions that would have made this story a compelling narrative, an entertaining and convincing story. Before exploring further her unusual educational experience and the meaning of Eunapius's description of her teachers, we should consider how the majority of girls of Sosipatra's social standing may have been educated at the time.

Education of Girls in Antiquity

Few girls in antiquity received more than a very rudimentary education if they received any at all. But girls of Sosipatra's class and social standing did so regularly. At the very least a private tutor would be hired to give elite girls training in grammar. But some girls would also receive further education in rhetoric and possibly even philosophy.[41] This was most often the case if the girl was the daughter of an intellectual or teacher.

41. Edward Jay Watts, *Hypatia: The Life and Legend of an Ancient Philosopher*, Women in Antiquity (New York: Oxford University Press, 2017), 22–23.

Some of these girls, such as Hypatia, the famous Alexandrian philosopher and mathematician, and a handful of others about whom we have very limited information, became teachers themselves, although this was rare. Their training was important regardless for a number of reasons. Women tended to marry considerably younger than men did. This meant that women often found themselves widowed at an age when their children still required someone to manage their education, to ensure they had suitable teachers as well as advantageous vocational opportunities.[42] These same women also had to manage households and estates after their husbands' deaths in the event a male relative or friend could not be relied upon to assist, a responsibility for which a basic education was helpful.

As mentioned, late ancient education was made up of three stages: grammatical, rhetorical, and philosophical training. Students could also study medicine, and students in philosophy schools were often exposed to biological and medical works as well as works of natural history. But young men, as well as women, could also become doctors by apprenticing with fathers, other relatives, or family friends.

Boys and girls would usually start their training in grammar at around the age of seven. In early adolescence, by about the age of thirteen, this grammatical training would be replaced with training in rhetoric.[43] This could be a gradual process with the same teacher, or it could involve a more abrupt shift to a new school, even one away from home with a new teacher. For instance, Eunapius went to Athens for his rhetorical training with Prohaeresius and then came back to Sardis to study philosophy with Chrysanthius. As a general rule, the "girls who began rhetorical training likely either completed or dropped out of it in their teens."[44]

Nonetheless, when we speak of grammar as a level in the ancient education system, we are speaking about much more than just learning how to read and write proper Greek. This is signaled by the manner of pedagogy at this level. Teachers taught students by reading texts together line by line. During these readings, teachers would pause to explain the significance of events and people. This significance could be moral, cosmological, metaphysical, theological, or literary. By means of this process, students would be inducted into a certain kind of worldview, a

---

42. Watts, *Hypatia* 21.
43. Watts, *Hypatia* 22.
44. Watts, *Hypatia* 23.

worldview shared with other elites across the Mediterranean who were also participating in the same kinds of readings of the same kinds of texts. This process made these elites recognizable to each other, capable of relating to each other far more readily than they might with people of different classes from their own regions.[45] The hermeneutical practice of elaborating on textual details in grammatical training is thereby representative of a general epistemological principle in Late Antiquity, one that also helps us to understand how Sosipatra's unique education fits in with late ancient modes of knowing and understanding the universe. This practice assumed that "careful reading of texts" would "enable careful reading of the cosmos."[46] In other words, "textual work is about knowing the cosmos, not the text alone."[47] Hence, "grammar can be taken here as a synonym for 'general knowledge of the order of things,' including language of textuality, but also familiarity with inherited texts, basic ethics, and the social and physical world."[48]

This expansive and totalizing understanding of education continued in the young person's rhetorical training, the next stage in the education process. This training most often took the form of exercises called *progymnasmata*, which "were supposed to teach a student how to write on set themes."[49]These exercises "were meant to warm up his muscles, stretch his power of discourse, and build his vigor."[50] A student would begin by "slavishly following a model, provided either by his own teacher or by a writer from the past"; over time he would become less dependent on these models as he honed his skills."[51] Many of the exercises assigned to students of rhetoric involved impersonation and "required a student to expand on the verbal reaction of a certain mythological or literary figure in a given situation."[52] Many girls who received grammatical training would not continue on with this sort of rhetorical training, much less full-fledged philosophical education. But some did follow this path.

45. Peter Brown, *Power and Persuasion in Late Antiquity: Towards a Christian Empire* (Madison: University of Wisconsin Press, 1992), 39.

46. Blossom Stefaniw, "Knowledge in Late Antiquity: What Is It Made of and What Does It Make?," *Studies in Late Antiquity* 2, no. 3 (September 1, 2018): 271.

47. Stefaniw, "Knowledge in Late Antiquity," 271.

48. Stefaniw, "Knowledge in Late Antiquity," 271.

49. Raffaella Cribiore, *Gymnastics of the Mind: Greek Education in Hellenistic and Roman Egypt* (Princeton, NJ: Princeton University Press, 2001), 221–22.

50. Cribiore, *Gymnastics of the Mind*, 222.

51. Cribiore, *Gymnastics of the Mind*, 221.

52. Cribiore, *Gymnastics of the Mind*, 228.

When it came to philosophical education, students and their parents had choices. They might choose a Stoic, Peripatetic, Platonic, or Epicurean school among others. Many teachers would introduce students to texts and ideas from a number of these traditions even though each teacher identified more specifically with one or another of these lineages. For instance, many Platonist teachers would have emphasized the close connections between the ideas of Plato and Pythagoras and would have also taught key works of Aristotle. As we know, the lineage Eunapius constructs and into which he embeds Sosipatra is a particular version of Platonism informed by contemporary interpretations of Pythagorean and Chaldean (i.e., ancient Babylonian) influences. And if we read Eunapius's entire biographical collection, we get a good sense of how these schools worked, including a sense of the networks of teachers and students that spread across the Eastern Mediterranean. Both rhetoric and philosophy teachers, especially for students who traveled away from home, often took on quasi-parental roles for their charges. And relationships developed between students that resembled those of siblings. This familial ethos was often purposefully cultivated as a way of inculcating loyalty and establishing networks that would be mutually beneficial for teachers and students in the future.[53]

Sosipatra's Unique Education

Sosipatra's education, as it is narrated by Eunapius, departs significantly from the pattern outlined above. First, its duration is comparatively very brief. It began when she was five and was completed by the time she was ten when, as we will see, her father returned to the estate. A young man who went through grammatical, rhetorical, and philosophical training would have been finished by his early or mid-twenties. Additionally, her teachers were mysterious itinerant workers who Eunapius suggests were likely to have been *daemones* or higher spirits. Their pedagogy consisted of a form of religious or ritual initiation and was so thorough in its effects that Sosipatra achieved a level of intellectual sophistication and comprehensive understanding that others might achieve only after years and years in all three levels of schooling.

---

53. Edward Jay Watts, *City and School in Late Antique Athens and Alexandria* (Berkeley: University of California Press, 2006), 11–14.

To grasp the precise ways in which Eunapius wishes his readers to understand the uniqueness of Sosipatra's education, it is necessary to focus on his discussion of its results. His discussion is also important because it introduces us to a whole worldview that must be unpacked and illuminated if we are to understand the point of Eunapius's story of Sosipatra instead of merely dismissing it as a complete fabrication. As mentioned in the introduction, Sosipatra's story is "serious entertainment," in other words, a story that intellectuals of Eunapius's circle and class would have enjoyed telling and hearing not only for the way it excited the imagination but for the larger philosophical and moral lessons it taught. It is that sense of the word "truth" that her story is meant to convey.

Eunapius describes the return of Sosipatra's father and the result of her five years spent under the care of her Chaldean guardians in the following manner. Her father returned to his estate at the appointed time, and he found her so changed as to be almost unrecognizable. Her teachers encouraged him at dinner to ask her whatever he wished in order to test the results of their tutelage. But she intervened and said, "Rather ask instead, father, what happened to you on the road."[54] She described his journey to him in accurate detail "as if she had been holding the reins," for he traveled in a four-wheeled carriage, a luxury conveyance that was prone to many calamities.[55] This is the same kind of vehicle that her kinsmen Philometer will have an accident in later in her life when she is a teacher at Pergamum, an event she views remotely as well. Sosipatra's father was amazed by her report and concluded that she must be a goddess. He begged her teachers to reveal to him who they were. They did so, only reluctantly, employing enigmatic words while "bowing their heads" and telling him they were not "uninitiated in the wisdom called Chaldean."[56] Believing he had truly encountered gods in the likeness of strangers, he called to mind the words of Homer: "And the gods, like unto strangers of foreign land, being in all shapes, do frequent cities."[57]

This idea, namely, that some human beings are really embodied daemons, heroes, or even gods, is one that was prevalent in the Neoplatonic tradition to which Eunapius belonged and had its roots

<hr>

54. Eunap., *VS* 6.66.
55. Eunap., *VS* 6.66.
56. Eunap., *VS* 6.68.
57. Eunap., *VS* 6.69. Homer, *Odyssey*, xvii.485.

in the *Chaldean Oracles* and the philosophy of Iamblichus.[58] Indeed, Iamblichus seems to have held the view that "the virtuous soul is said to be rewarded by becoming an angel after death."[59] But also that "these angels then redescend to earth and reincarnate into new bodies."[60] They do so for two purposes: "First, by serving as teachers, they help others perfect their souls. Second, by redescending into materiality, they participate in the demiurge's continual re-creation and re-ordering of the material world."[61] We see in the story of Sosipatra's relationship with the two Chaldeans that they do both of these things. They teach her and initiate her into their mysteries, thereby perfecting her soul. But they also manage her father's estate in a superior fashion, including tending the vines. In this respect, they were fulfilling the obligation of the theurgist to "discover the proper ways in which material objects such as plants and stones could be manipulated so as to help sustain, promote, and enhance cosmic re-creation."[62]

Hence, Eunapius is implying that Sosipatra's teachers are reincarnated souls of daemons, angels, or even higher divinities. And his initial reference to their ages, namely, that despite both being old, they were not the same age, may have been his way of hinting to his readers that these two were, in fact, the reincarnated souls of the two Juliani, the legendary authors, father and son, of the *Chaldean Oracles*.[63]

Their divine identity is further emphasized by the details of their departure. Despite the fact that Sosipatra's father beseeched the two teachers to remain and continue their work with his daughter, they secretly prepared to leave. They handed over to Sosipatra her initiation garments, various instruments, and also some small books, all of which were put into her chest.[64] This chest may have been similar to that which other elite girls possessed as a kind of "hope chest" with which to play matron of the household. In her case, the contents signal that she is prepared for much more than a domestic future. The two then

---

58. The *Chaldean Oracles*, as discussed in more detail later in the book, was a text written

59. Sarah Iles Johnston, "Working Overtime in the Afterlife; or, No Rest for the Virtuous," in *Heavenly Realms and Earthly Realities in Late Antique Religions*, ed. Annette Yoshiko Reed and Ra'anan S. Boustan (Cambridge: Cambridge University Press, 2004), 88.

60. Johnston, "Working Overtime in the Afterlife," 88.

61. Johnston, "Working Overtime in the Afterlife," 88.

62. Johnston, "Working Overtime in the Afterlife," 97.

63. Henriette Harich-Schwarzbauer, "Das Seelengefährt in Der Lehre Der Theurgin Sosipatra (Eunapios VPS 466,5,1-471,9,17)," *Archaiognosia. Supplement* 8 (2009): 64.

64. Eunap., *VS* 6.70.

told Sosipatra that they would be traveling to the Western Ocean, which would have also signaled that they were blessed spirits.[65]

The story of the remarkable results of Sosipatra's education by *daemones* and their subsequent departure for higher realms presents us with a number of interesting historiographical challenges and some very fascinating information that helps to explain the thought world of Eunapius and his colleagues, even if it does little to inform us about how a girl of her social class would have normally been educated. Hence, our task is to explore how such an education was possible in the mind of someone such as Eunapius and how this story would have been heard at the time.

First, we can most simply and clearly state that for Eunapius and most other ancient intellectuals, education was thought to be transformational. In the case of the Iamblichan lineage, it was thought to be divinizing. Sosipatra is barely recognizable to her father and he thinks of her as a goddess when he sees her after his five-year absence. Eunapius does not mention that her teachers taught her anything in particular. Rather, the only activity he mentions is her initiation into certain mysteries and rites all of which remained a secret between the three of them. For theurgists, initiation into religious mysteries was a form of education in secret forms of *sophia*. In the *Lives*, Eunapius records the rites into which other of his subjects are initiated along with details about their educational paths, demonstrating there is a clear link in his mind. In the case of Sosipatra, there is no mention of lessons, readings, or exercises. And the books her teachers gave her upon their departure were sealed in a chest, rendering them unreadable.

Eunapius continues his story by relating that from the time her teachers departed, Sosipatra's father permitted her to live as she wished. The only thing about her that he found at all vexing was her tendency to remain silent. Her silence is in keeping with her divine status and devotion to higher truths, which she shares only when prompted or inspired by superior spirits. In other words, Eunapius is building a picture of her as an oracle of sorts, even at this early stage in her life. When she did communicate, however, "she had on her lips the books of the poets, philosophers, and orators."[66] And she was able to explain everything she

65. Eunap., *VS* 6.73.
66. Eunap., *VS* 6.75.

said with ease, truths which others "amidst labor and hard work, could only begin to barely and indistinctly understand."[67]

When we read this description, we might assume that Eunapius is juxtaposing how Sosipatra came to know and fully comprehend all the works of the poets, philosophers, and orators with the usual path students would follow to gain such knowledge, the path of hard work and painful drudgery. We know of this path from other contexts, namely, the descriptions of writers such as Augustine, Libanius, and Ausonius, to name a few. Indeed, late ancient education "often proved physically and emotionally draining." The method of learning, particularly the memorization of texts, "consumed immense amounts of time and energy."[68] And yet, we might more accurately say that Eunapius is placing Sosipatra's education on the ideal end of a continuum of educational practices, processes, and outcomes. The ease with which Sosipatra and her teachers achieve the same results, that is, complete mastery of the poets, philosophers, and orators, tells us something about how Eunapius thinks of the ideal education in terms of the ideal student, ideal teachers, and ideal curriculum. Indeed, the curriculum is really the static element in this picture. It would have been mastered more or less completely in the case of distinct pedagogical relationships between students and teachers. Eunapius means to imply that Sosipatra's mastery is complete. And it is not just a mastery of texts but also a kind of mastery of cosmic or universal knowledge reflected in the authoritative texts he alludes to in his phrase "the works of the poets, philosophers, and orators."

The completeness of Sosipatra's mastery of all of this knowledge is predicated on the superiority of her soul, a point Eunapius makes by alluding to her divinity in many places in his account of her life. Implicit in his description of Sosipatra's beauty, charm, and aptitude is the understanding that her soul has descended from a superior part of the cosmos and is capable of further perfection and transformation during her life on earth. The cosmos gives her ideal teachers for this purpose, being divine spirits themselves. Instead of teaching her in the manner of ordinary grammarians and teachers of rhetoric or philosophy, they initiate her into mysteries that unlock the secrets of the cosmos for her, so she can know and understand in the manner of a god, without the limitations of sense experience. In other words, her manner of knowing

---

67. Eunap., *VS* 6.75.

68. Watts, *The Final Pagan Generation*, 52.

is not limited by her embodiment. This kind of knowing is anticipated in the works of earlier Platonists and runs through the Iamblichan lineage. It is also represented in contemporary Christian thought such as the works of Origen of Alexandria and his heirs, as well as in so-called Gnostic texts. This way of thinking about knowledge and the provisional nature of embodiment and its limits means that even within the category "human being" there was a great deal of ontological flexibility and variability. Many kinds of souls could appear in human form and inhabit human bodies. Humans could live the life of both angels and beasts. Sosipatra followed the transformational example of her divine teachers and lived a more divine sort of existence. Her ability to see her father's journey remotely signals her ability to transcend the limits of embodied knowledge.

How do we make sense of the curriculum Sosipatra has mastered through her initiation? Is it that Sosipatra has learned something importantly different from other students? Or has she learned the same things that make up the curriculum of late ancient education but in a more complete and total manner? Given Eunapius's statement that she is able to quote from memory the works of the poets, philosophers, and orators and explain them easily, it must be the latter. But what then is the significance of her mysterious initiations if what she ends up knowing is what other elite educated children would know by other more painful and arduous means?

Eunapius participates in a certain understanding of both knowledge and the cosmos that makes the difference in degree in this case of critical importance. We can take the example of Homer or of Egyptian myths as a point of departure. As early as Plutarch (c. 46–c. 120 CE) and other Middle Platonic writers (second and third centuries CE), we observe a tendency to read myth figurally or allegorically, as revealing deeper philosophical truths about the cosmos. Plutarch's reading of the myth of Isis and Osiris in his *Moralia* is a good example of this phenomenon. He interprets the elements of the myth as a kind of allegory for universal Platonic truths about the soul and the gods. He prefaces his commentary on the myth with a lengthy discussion of the habits of the Egyptian priesthood, explaining the philosophical principles that he thinks must inform their abstention from certain foods, their dress, and style of life. In a similar manner, Porphyry's exegeses of Homeric myths are examples of this interpretive tendency. And Origen is the one who makes most explicit a similar kind of hermeneutical schema for reading

Hebrew scripture and the Christian Gospels. This kind of reading of texts mirrors the way in which philosophers in Late Antiquity thought about reading the cosmos more generally. Many of them assumed that the "cosmos has its own legibility and as such is both structured like a text and structures all the texts which purport to represent it."[69]

Sosipatra can merely possess important texts sealed up in her chest, because she has already been trained to and initiated into an ability to read the cosmos itself. Eunapius implies that she has a kind of total knowledge that allows her to apprehend the truths of texts in their deepest sense as they reflect cosmic truths. She has assimilated herself to divinity, to the highest levels of the cosmos whence she can view things in all their interconnectedness. This kind of knowing also makes possible the "opportunity to act in and modify the world through the conscious application of the world's own patterns. This knowing is a practical, political, and indeed physical engagement."[70]

We find many examples of this understanding of knowing in late ancient literature. For instance, in Iamblichus's *On the Pythagorean Way of Life*, Pythagoras is reported to have been able to heal his sick students and followers by playing music for them.[71] This works, because health is understood as bodily harmony, a proportional harmony of the four humors, and music is also a proportional harmony in Pythagorean thought. Indeed, music is, in its essence, mathematical, and the music Pythagoras would have produced, on Iamblichus's reading, would have served as a microcosmic image of the music the planets made as they moved in their orbits around the earth. This view of the cosmos as a singular totality implies that everything in it is "enchained" such that the goal of cosmological knowledge is "the uncovering of the singular rationality that governed the connections and resemblances between the different agents and elements in the universe."[72]

Philosophers and others who grappled with cosmology in Late Antiquity, among whom we can easily place the thinkers in Eunapius's biographies, "followed their predecessors in assuming a general principle of sympathy between all the parts of this visible and invisible world

---

69. Stefaniw, "Knowledge in Late Antiquity," 271.

70. C. M. Chin and Moulie Vidas, eds., *Late Ancient Knowing: Explorations in Intellectual History* (Oakland: University of California Press, 2015), 6.

71. Iamb. *VP*, 25.110–11.

72. Chin and Vidas, *Late Ancient Knowing*, 6–7.

that, in their order, are the cosmos."[73] Plotinus referred to this doctrine of sympathy by asserting that all things must be "enchained" and "the sympathy and correspondence obtaining in any one closely knit organism must exist, first, and most intensely, in the All."[74] This view of the cosmos is not just metaphysical; it is also "mundane."[75] This means that even though cosmological knowledge could operate at the highest intellectual level, as was the case with thinkers such as Plotinus and Origen, "the principle of universal correspondence" could also be used to explain "the flourishing of sympathetic practices sometimes called magic, sometimes called *technē*, sometimes called astrology, and sometimes called worship."[76] This helps to explain how a philosopher such as Sosipatra could be initiated into mysteries as part of her experience of ancient Greek *paideia* (i.e., standard rhetorical and philosophical education); it also explains her ability to see remotely. It also explains her teachers' ability to cause grapevines and little girls both to flourish to their fullest potential.

If we are to understand the world into which Eunapius writes Sosipatra and the particular moments he records of her life, it helps if we understand that we must grasp three principles about the ancient worldview:

> first, that events are shaped by external invisible forces; second,
> that events and actions are necessarily the products of multiple
> interacting agents, only some of whom are human; and third,
> that all things, human and nonhuman, visible and invisible,
> seek to be brought into accord.[77]

At this point, we begin to see how Eunapius's stories about Sosipatra fit into this much larger worldview, a worldview shared by a large number of late ancient intellectuals, non-Christian polytheists, Christian theologians, Jewish rabbis, and others. Although Sosipatra was not educated like most other children in her day, she came to know a canon of authorities, or what we might call the "patrimony" of antiquity, that

---

73. C. M. Chin, "Cosmos," in *Late Ancient Knowing: Explorations in Intellectual History*, ed. C. M. Chin and Moulie Vidas (Berkeley: University of California Press, 2015), 99.

74. This passage from Plotinus, *Enneads* 2.3–7, is quoted by Chin, "Cosmos," 99. The translation is by Stephan MacKenna.

75. Chin, "Cosmos," 100.

76. Chin, "Cosmos," 100.

77. Chin, "Cosmos," 100–101.

made her recognizable to other members of her social class.[78] And even though her teachers were thought to be divine spirits, there are no striking differences between how Eunapius describes them and the way he describes some of his own beloved teachers and other philosophers in his work. Education in this Platonic lineage ideally meant assimilation to the cosmos in general and to divinity in particular.

As we transition in Chapter 3 to a discussion of Sosipatra's life as a married woman, mother, and widow, it is interesting to note that in Christian contexts, for a young woman to experience this kind of assimilation to divinity and transformation through proper *paideia*, she would have had to undertake an ascetic life, one in which, to use the language of hagiographers and other early Christian writers, she would have had to become male. She would have given up the traditional path of marriage and childbearing and childrearing. In Eunapius's telling, Sosipatra attains the highest intellectual achievements possible in his account of the philosophical life, and she does so without this sort of ascetic renunciation. In this respect, Eunapius may have been using his image of Sosipatra to respond to Christian hagiographies of female saints in the form of what we might call competitive biography.

78. Stefaniw, "Knowledge in Late Antiquity," 271–74.

3

Sosipatra as a Wife, Mother, and Widow

We can begin this chapter, like the last one, with another image, the image found on many sarcophagi and funerary stele of a couple holding right hands or embracing.[1] In some instances, the goddess Concordia joins the couple by placing her hands around their shoulders (Figure 3.1). Concordia here symbolizes a sense of shared harmony in marriage. It is an idealized image, like the image of a girl with doves, one of marital harmony and familial happiness.[2] It is perhaps tinged with less sadness than the funerary stele commemorating a girl who died in her youth before she could experience the ideal and anticipated pleasures and joys of married life. But this ideal image would have also, in many cases, misrepresented the reality of many Greco-Roman marriages given factors such as patriarchy, misogyny, domestic abuse, the dangers of childbirth, high infant mortality rates, the difference in sexual mores between married men and women, especially in the context of slave-owning families, and so forth, However, in Eunapius's account, Sosipatra's marriage to Eustathius aligned in important respects with the ideal of marital concord. At the same time, however, it departed from certain norms in terms of Sosipatra's degree of agency in choosing when and whom she would marry. Furthermore, Sosipatra and Eustathius may have separated, or Eustathius may have abandoned his family, a detail that might disrupt the otherwise ideal portrait of our subject.[3]

1. For a beautiful example of this image, see the photo of the Sarcophagus with scenes of the life of a Roman military officer from the Palazzo Ducale at Mantua at the following link: http://ancientrome.ru/art/artworken/img.htm?id=4262.

2. Karen K. Hersch, *The Roman Wedding: Ritual and Meaning in Antiquity* (New York: Cambridge University Press, 2010), 209–11.

3. Both Garth Fowden and Robert J. Penella have suggested these possibilities, which we discuss later in this chapter.

Sosipatra of Pergamum. Heidi Marx, Oxford University Press (2021). © Oxford University Press.
DOI: 10.1093/oso/9780190618858.003.0003

FIGURE 3.1 Sarcophagus with a matrimonial scene, Concordia encircles the couple with her arms, marble, third century CE. Inv. No. A 433, Saint Petersburg, State Hermitage Museum. Photo by Ilia Shurygin, 2012; information from museum annotation; used with permission of the photographer.

In this chapter, we will explore what Sosipatra's late adolescent/early adult life might have been like from her betrothal to Eustathius to the time when she began teaching in Pergamum. This chapter will discuss what family life would have been like for someone such as Sosipatra. It will endeavor to answer questions such as what would her household responsibilities have been, what were the difficulties and dangers she may have faced in the course of bringing her children into the world and bringing them up, what role might she have played in their education, and so forth. We are fortunate to have a rich scholarship on these topics, allowing us to sketch a picture of what Sosipatra's married and family life may have been like. We are also able to draw interesting comparisons with Christian women who chose to remain celibate or who convinced their husbands to live chastely after they had brought a number of children into the world, and women who, like Sosipatra, had considerable wealth and property at their disposal. And if she and Eustathius did part ways at a certain point, she also provides an interesting opportunity for thinking about single motherhood in Late Antiquity. Once again Eunapius gives us very little detail to work with, just a few lines and a couple of tantalizing vignettes. Hence, our task will be to fill in with what we know from the late ancient eastern Empire about adolescence, betrothal, marriage, childbirth and childrearing, and widowhood in order to weave a plausible picture for our subjects.

Female Adolescence in Late Antiquity

We lose track of Sosipatra's specific age when she is ten years old, after she has completed her five years of initiation with her daemonic teachers. And we do not know her age when she married, so it is impossible to draw comparisons between her life path and that of her peers. But we can offer plausible speculation on a range of possibilities. And we can certainly consider what the transition from girlhood to adulthood might have been like in the case of other women from Sosipatra's time period and social class.

Although some scholarship has dismissed or downplayed a "period of female youth" in Greco-Roman antiquity as a result of the "apparently early age of marriage," there is good reason to believe that girls, similar to boys, experienced a form of adolescence as a life stage.[4] For instance, epigraphic evidence shows that for "females who died under the age of twenty, parents were normally the commemorators," which means that even though the legal minimum age for marriage was twelve, most

---

4. Lisa A. Alberici and Mary Harlow, "Age and Innocence: Female Transitions to Adulthood in Late Antiquity," *Hesperia Supplements* 41 (2007): 194.

women married in their late teens.[5] In elite families, because of the concern for maintaining wealth and property, girls did tend to marry at an earlier age.[6] By law, then, Sosipatra could have chosen to marry from the age of twelve on. But as "the mean age of first marriage among upper-class girls in the empire has been estimated to be in the late teens," it is likely that she waited a number of years before marrying.[7]

The other kind of evidence we can use to establish a period of female adolescence in antiquity is medical literature from writers such as Galen, Soranus, and Oribasius (a contemporary of Sosipatra's and the close advisor and doctor to Emperor Julian). The fact that these writers address this period in young women's lives specifically and develop distinct regimens for it suggests "that it was anticipated as an extended period."[8] The main aim of these regimens was to control sexual desire so as to guarantee chastity and virginity at the time of marriage: "It was important not only to control the development of young girls but also to be seen to be doing so."[9] Medical literature reflects the "cultural expectations of youthful femininity" in this respect and emphasizes "the preservation of sexual purity until marriage and the belief that female passions began to become unruly at puberty."[10] We have an example from Soranus suggesting that young girls might be subjected to the following regimen from thirteen years of age:

> Therefore, her walk should be easy and deliberate, passive
> exercise and prolonged gymnastics not forced, much fat
> applied in the massage, a bath taken daily, and the mind
> diverted in every possible way.[11]

That Sosipatra's family or guardians felt the need to impose such a regimen on her as she entered puberty seems unlikely given her temperament and her tendency to have her mind ever diverted by philosophy and literature anyway. Nor does Eunapius give the impression that Sosipatra would have been subject to "unruly passions" in puberty. But other parents of her class may well have followed the advice of medical

5. Alberici and Harlow, "Age and Innocence," 194.

6. Alberici and Harlow, "Age and Innocence," 195. See also Lauren E. Caldwell, *Roman Girlhood and the Fashioning of Femininity* (Cambridge: Cambridge University Press, 2015).

7. Caldwell, *Roman Girlhood*, 3.

8. Alberici and Harlow, "Age and Innocence," 195.

9. Alberici and Harlow, "Age and Innocence," 197.

10. Caldwell, *Roman Girlhood*, 6.

11. Sor., *Gyn.* 1.4.25. Quoted in Alberici and Harlow, "Age and Innocence," 197.

manuals or consulted with doctors such as Oribasius on how best to preserve their daughters' virginity until they married.

We might also ask whether Sosipatra marked the transition from childhood to womanhood in any ritual way. As we discussed in Chapter 2 regarding Sosipatra's possible participation in civic and household worship of traditional Mediterranean divinities, it is safe to assume that in the early and mid–fourth century, religious ritual in Asia Minor was characterized by a great deal of continuity with the previous couple of centuries.[12] And given the nature of Iamblichan theurgy and its theology of ritual, participating in festivals and private worships would have been a reasonable, even a desirable, thing to do. Hence, as Sosipatra moved from childhood into adolescence and womanhood, she likely dedicated her toys or clothes in the temple of a female deity as a sign of gratitude and of hope for a certain kind of future, one with a family of her own. She may, in fact, have done so at the Temple of Artemis at Ephesus.[13]

Betrothal and Marriage in Late Antiquity

As mentioned in an earlier chapter, Eunapius introduces the story of Sosipatra as a substantial digression from his account of Eustathius, a digression that in fact plays a central role in his overall narrative in terms of the way it presents his readers with an image of a non-Christian holy woman, an image that could engage competitively with contemporary images of female Christian saints. In introducing Sosipatra to his readers, Eunapius writes: "Well then, the great Eustathius married Sosipatra, who proved through the superiority of her wisdom that her husband was inferior and insignificant."[14]

From the outset, we should note that what is unique about Sosipatra's betrothal and marriage is the claim that she chose Eustathius, and not that he was chosen for her by her father. Not only is this out of the ordinary in terms of common practice for elite families in this time period, as we will see in a moment, but it also leaves us with a

---

12. Fritz Graf, *Roman Festivals in the Greek East: From the Early Empire to the Middle Byzantine Era* (Cambridge: Cambridge University Press, 2015).

13. Cecilie Brøns, *Gods and Garments: Textiles in Greek Sanctuaries in the 7th–1st Centuries BC* (Oxford: Oxbow Books, 2016). See Brøns, Appendix 4, for evidence of garment pins left as votives in the temple.

14. Eunap., *VS* 6.53.

number of unanswered questions: How did Sosipatra know or know of Eustathius? How old was Sosipatra when she made her decision to marry? How old was Eustathius? Was Sosipatra's father still alive when she chose to marry? If not, who was her guardian? Was she in love with Eustathius? In other words, what was behind her choice? With respect to the final question, we need to be conscious of how people in antiquity might have thought about the relationship between being in love as we think about it today and marriage. As we will see when we discuss an episode during her widowhood where a kinsman, Philometer, casts a love spell on Sosipatra, our notions of falling in love and getting married as a matter of individual choice don't necessarily map onto those informing Eunapius's telling of Sosipatra's story in particular, nor onto those informing ideas about marriage more generally in Late Antiquity. That being said, some scholars have noted a shift in this period from thinking of marriage as a civic duty to thinking of it more in terms of individual choice.[15]

All that Eunapius tells us is that at a certain moment, Sosipatra decided to wed, and "it was indisputable that Eustathius alone of all men was worthy of marriage to her."[16] We might ask why Eustathius was the only suitable candidate for her. One way of answering this question is by focusing on where he was situated in the Iamblichan philosophical lineage. Eustathius was a student of Aedesius (and possibly of Iamblichus himself). Eustathius was also a kinsman of Aedesius, which means that Sosipatra became related to Aedesius and came to inhabit the Iamblichan lineage through marriage in addition to her knowledge of Chaldean wisdom and the canon of late Platonist schools.

Although the story of Sosipatra's engagement to Eustathius is somewhat out of the ordinary, her choice still accords with most societal expectations governing female behavior at the time: "In general, philosophically-minded women did their duty to family and city by marrying philosophically-minded men and bearing children."[17] Their unions were ideally meant to uphold "the moral qualities of both parties" and thereby "reveal an ideal of marriage as a well-planned partnership

15. Mathew Kuefler, "The Marriage Revolution in Late Antiquity: The Theodosian Code and Later Roman Marriage Law," *Journal of Family History* 32, no. 4 (October 1, 2007): 345.

16. Wilmer Cave Wright, *Philostratus and Eunapius: The Lives of the Sophists* (Cambridge, MA: Harvard University Press, 1989), 76.

17. Gillian Clark, *Monica: An Ordinary Saint*, Women in Antiquity (New York: Oxford University Press, 2015), 93.

intended to produce children to whom moral values as well as family name and property are to be transmitted."[18] Even Porphyry, student of Plotinus (who did not take a wife), married a widow to ensure that her children were not left without resources, both financial and philosophical. The true exceptions were women such as Hypatia in Alexandria, a non-Christian philosopher, and Macrina in Cappadocia, a Christian ascetic, women who chose not to marry but who clearly chose to live philosophical lives. In the aforementioned philosophically oriented families, husbands ideally undertook their civic duties "without ambition or display" and these marriages "linked the families of philosophers."[19] We certainly see this kind of intermarriage in Eunapius's biographies.

If Sosipatra is unusual in her decision to choose her own suitor and marry, we might ask what the normal situation might have been for an elite girl in her mid to late teens. Other young women of Sosipatra's age and class would have had marriages arranged for them by their families, whether by their fathers, their male guardians if their fathers had died, or their widowed mothers if these women retained guardianship. These betrothals could and often did take place prior to the age at which girls could legally marry, namely twelve. For instance, Augustine's mother, Monica, arranged a betrothal for him when he was in his thirties to a ten-year-old girl for whom he had to wait two years. It was to be a financially advantageous match, for which Augustine abandoned his partner of fourteen years and mother of his son, Adeodatus.[20]

Generally, men first married later in life than women, the men being anywhere from their late twenties to their fifties or even sixties. There is reason to believe that Eustathius was older than Sosipatra at the time of their marriage. For instance, at the time of their wedding, she predicted that they would have three children together and that he would die after five years. We will discuss this prophetic activity in its own right in the final chapter of the book. And as I mentioned earlier, there is some scholarly confusion about the timing of Eustathius's death relative to this prophesy and to some of the details Eunapius relates about the life of their son, Antoninus. But it is reasonable to assume that if Eustathius did die after five years of marriage to Sosipatra that he was somewhat older than she was. This pattern of older men marrying younger women

18. Judith Evans Grubbs, *Law and Family in Late Antiquity: The Emperor Constantine's Marriage Legislation* (Oxford: Clarendon Press, 1995), 58–59.

19. Clark, *Monica*, 93.

20. Aug., *Conf.*, 6.13–25.

seems not to have changed in Late Antiquity. In "economies with land-based wealth" a man often has to wait until his father's death and an inheritance to be able to access the means to support a family, "whereas women tend to marry as soon as they reach child-bearing age."[21] Hence, it is likely that Eustathius was older, possibly considerably older, than Sosipatra.

The process of betrothal in this period usually involved some form of gift from the man to his future wife, in addition to the usual arrangements related to the dowry that the future wife would bring with her into the marriage. This practice was, in fact, more frequent in Late Antiquity.[22] The wife kept this gift. In other words, it didn't pass into her father's hands. But she was also "forbidden to sell it or otherwise alienate it and had to preserve it for her children."[23] This gift may have become more important than the dowry that women brought to their marriages. Additionally, extravagant gifts between husbands and wives after marriage were prohibited by law.[24] So betrothal and marriage were the time when any large gifts had to be made.

A dowry in Late Antiquity was a "transfer of money or property from the wife's family of birth to the married couple." "Income from the money or property belonged to the husband, but the dowry itself continued to belong to the wife's paterfamilias or her other blood relatives, so her husband could not sell land that was part of a dowry."[25] Dowries would revert to a woman at her husband's death instead of becoming part of his family's inheritance.[26]

Between the betrothal gift from the future husband and the dowry of the future wife, which was also importantly inalienable, it meant that "both a husband's and a wife's families contributed to the financial independence of the couple."[27] This is germane to Sosipatra's situation given her husband's death early in their marriage, because it also meant that "a widow had more resources at her disposal with lands and income from both the dowry and the betrothal gifts that could not be taken from her by a former husband's family."[28] This may also explain why many elite

21. Kuefler, "The Marriage Revolution in Late Antiquity," 351.
22. Kuefler, "The Marriage Revolution in Late Antiquity," 352–53.
23. Kuefler, "The Marriage Revolution in Late Antiquity," 353.
24. Kuefler, "The Marriage Revolution in Late Antiquity," 354.
25. Kuefler, "The Marriage Revolution in Late Antiquity," 352.
26. Kuefler, "The Marriage Revolution in Late Antiquity," 352.
27. Kuefler, "The Marriage Revolution in Late Antiquity," 354.
28. Kuefler, "The Marriage Revolution in Late Antiquity," 354.

widows chose not to remarry. The one limit on use of these resources was that a widow was "obliged to preserve both forms of marriage payment for her children."[29]

In the case of Sosipatra's marriage, we have no way of knowing what each party brought to the union in terms of land, wealth, and other movable goods. We can assume that the combined resources of this particular couple, however, allowed for a comfortable existence. The only actual properties Eunapius speaks about in his narratives of the lives of Eustathius and Sosipatra are Aedesius's property in Cappadocia which Eustathius managed for him and Sosipatra's property, possibly more than one, in Asia Minor, including a dwelling in Pergamum, to which she returned upon her husband's death and in which she housed her school of philosophy. We do not know whether she inherited the estate on which she received her education, nor do we know what became of any urban dwellings her father may have owned. In addition to property, Sosipatra would have brought other kinds of movable goods into her marriage as part of her dowry, including jewelry, household textiles, clothing, cookware, utensils, furniture, sums of money, and possibly slaves.[30]

In terms of process or actions taken and traditions followed—in other words, betrothal, dowry, marriage contract and ceremony, and so forth—we can assume some continuity between Sosipatra and her contemporaries. When it came to the nuptials themselves, no written contract or ceremony was necessary in antiquity. In the case, however, of wealthy families, there was usually some sort of written record "attesting the marriage and recording the dowry" and betrothal gift.[31] The validity of marriage was quite simply based "on the desire of both parties to be married and on the absence of any hindrances to marriage, such as prohibitions based on kinship or social status."[32] This latter point was important. Only Roman citizens could marry each other. Other social classes could cohabitate. But marital relations with "persons of widely differing social classes" were prohibited.[33]

We can also assume that there was some sort of ceremony or celebration of Sosipatra's marriage to Eustathius. Indeed, Eunapius suggests

29. Kuefler, "The Marriage Revolution in Late Antiquity," 354.
30. Evans Grubbs, *Law and Family in Late Antiquity*, 146.
31. Evans Grubbs, *Law and Family in Late Antiquity*, 142.
32. Evans Grubbs, *Law and Family in Late Antiquity*, 153.
33. Kuefler, "The Marriage Revolution in Late Antiquity," 349.

that it is at this celebration that Sosipatra prophetically announced the number of children they would have, when her husband would die, and where his soul would reside after his death.

It is hard to know in any detail what kind of ceremony Sosipatra and Eustathius may have participated in at the time of their wedding. We have accounts of much earlier Greek wedding rituals and also information about Roman rites. But in Asia Minor in Late Antiquity, it is difficult to discern how rituals may have evolved. For instance, Sosipatra may have taken a purificatory bath as the bride. After this she may have put on special clothes, even ones which she herself wove. Having adorned herself, she may have processed with her family to her husband's home, which may have also been decorated in some special and celebratory way. He may have carried her over the threshold, a Roman tradition that may have been adopted in the Greek East at some point. Finally, the household may have gathered to perform some sort of ritual of incorporation around the family hearth or altar.

Married Life in Late Antiquity

Eunapius does not provide us with any details about Sosipatra's marriage to Eustathius beyond describing the length of his life and the number of sons they had together. Depending on her age when she married, she was likely widowed or separated from Eustathius very young. Other information we lack leads us to wonder if Sosipatra settled with her new husband in Cappadocia where he was, at one time, managing Aedesius's estate. If so, did she participate in that management as mistress of the household? Did she then move to Pergamum from Cappadocia or from some other location? If Eustathius was in imperial administration, for instance, did the couple ever live in Constantinople or any other regional capital? Whatever the case may have been, geography notwithstanding, we can sketch some of the likely realities that would have defined her domestic and marital existence and some of the activities that would have made up her days.

For Sosipatra to have had three sons in five years, she and Eustathius likely made an immediate start on trying to conceive. This would not have been unusual, given the emphasis placed on having children and the demographic realities that required women to bear, on average, 5.87

children to replace the population.[34] Their life together reveals none of the qualms and reservations on the part of either partner exhibited by certain Christian elite women around these matters, women such as Melania the Younger who attempted to persuade her husband Pinian to remain chaste in their arranged marriage. Pinian insisted on having two children before yielding to his wife's wishes. Tragically both children died at very young ages. The couple then decided to pursue a shared life of chastity, having at least attempted to fulfill their societal duty. Sosipatra was far more fortunate. She had three sons, all of whom survived into adulthood, and at least one survived her death, namely, Antoninus. We will discuss the realities of conception and childbirth shortly, but for now suffice it to say that Sosipatra and Eustathius seemed content to conform to a very pro-cultural understanding of ancient marriage.

As a result of the spread of Christianity, women in the fourth century had a number of interesting new vocations and life paths open to them. The main choice they could make was between traditional marriage and celibacy. In the case of the latter, they could choose to join an establishment for virgins of various sorts: live in their family homes; band together with other virgins in smaller, more informal groups; or even live with a man who had made a similar kind of vow (an option the Archbishop of Antioch, John Chrysostom, heartily disapproved of and maligned). In light of these new Christian lifestyle choices, it is telling that Eunapius's heroine follows the very traditional Greco-Roman path of marriage and motherhood.

The realities of a typical marriage were often far from fair or pleasant for women. We aren't given any information that would trouble an idealized picture of *Concordia* between Sosipatra and Eustathius, except that they may have separated. But other women of her class could reasonably expect that their husbands might abandon their marriage bed for the slave quarters on occasion, even producing children from these encounters. The same freedoms, however, were not extended to wives, who could be punished, at times brutally, for sexual infidelity with household slaves. And were one to have the misfortune of having married a husband with a temper, which he failed to control in good Stoic fashion, a wife could also expect physical abuse. Augustine, in his *Confessions*, describes the advice Monica, his mother, gave to other women exhibiting the signs of such domestic abuse in order to help

---

34. Caldwell, *Roman Girlhood*, 6.

them avoid similar treatment in the future. Her advice was essentially to put up and shut up. And she implies that she herself had to suffer in silence the philandering and abuse of her own husband, Augustine's father.[35] Given the fact that Sosipatra is described as having chosen the only man worthy of her, it is no wonder we do not hear about marital discord between them. But she would have been a rare exception given sexual mores of the day and the power differences between men and women in the ancient world more generally. Furthermore, if Eustathius did abandon her, or they separated, whether amicably or on account of conflict, Eunapius was either unaware of the circumstances or chose not to air the couple's "dirty laundry" in his idealized report.

Practical Household Management

In the Roman East, brides generally went to live with the groom's family. If her mother-in-law was still alive, the bride would have been under this woman's authority and may have been expected to do a good deal of "grunt work" until she bore children of her own.[36] In Sosipatra's case, we know nothing about the circumstances into which she married. Whether or not she had to conduct the exercise of her household duties under the watchful, even critical, gaze of Eustathius's mother, we can assume that on the basis of her education, she would have been more than capable of managing in an exemplary fashion the affairs of an urban home or rural estate or possibly both. After all, she understood the principles that ordered the cosmos, so we can deduce from Eunapius's laudatory narrative that she would not have failed to apply those principles when ordering and managing her own household, just as her teachers had done vis-à-vis her father's estate. In the case of other, more "ordinary" young girls from families of means, we know that they would have been socialized to take on roles in household management from an early age.[37] Some of them would have even had their own little chest in the

35. Aug., *Conf.*, 9.9. Gillian Clark discusses many of these stark realities in her portrait of Monica, Augustine's mother: Clark, *Monica*, 58–64.

36. Mona Tokarek LaFosse, "Age Hierarchy and Social Networks among Urban Women in the Roman East," in *Mediterranean Families in Antiquity: Households, Extended Families, and Domestic Space*, ed. Sabine R. Huebner and Geoffrey S. Nathan (Chichester, West Sussex: Wiley Blackwell, 2017), 209.

37. According to Gillian Clark, some of our best sources of information on the tasks women performed in the home and for the household are treatises on virginity that aimed to persuade girls and their parents that domestic life was drudgery and that childbearing and childrearing was

storeroom and a key with which they could play house.[38] In addition to her preparedness and skills, Sosipatra's social class likely afforded plenty of competent help.

If Sosipatra and Eustathius had considerable landholdings between them, they would have overseen the provisioning of their household directly from what was produced by their estates. What they could not provide for themselves, they would have purchased, perhaps using funds generated by selling surplus goods of, for instance, wine or agricultural produce, but also finished goods produced by slaves and other workers. Some of these goods, woven items, for instance, may have even been produced by the women of the household and Sosipatra herself.[39] Recall that Sosipatra's father's estate was involved in viniculture. Some wives would have even overseen the sale of goods independent of their husband's involvement or direction. Again, we do not know what kinds of activities Sosipatra took on in her role as wife and household manager. But she would have been quite capable of participating in accounting and high-level decision making based on Eunapius's general description of her knowledge and virtues. Her education by Chaldeans and her likely familiarity with Iamblichan philosophy, which was a hybridization of Platonism and Pythagoreanism, implies that she had extensive mathematical knowledge. After all, Plato argued that students of philosophy should study mathematics first in order to train the soul to contemplate abstract reality. And the Chaldeans were famous for astrological expertise, which depended on a thorough grounding in mathematical knowledge. We can also think of Hypatia in this regard, who taught mathematics in Alexandria. And as mentioned in Chapter 2, young girls were given a rudimentary training in mathematics precisely to prepare them for their household duties. Sosipatra's knowledge of astronomy and mathematics would have possibly allowed her to predict agricultural outcomes in a manner similar to the Ionian philosopher Thales, who was purported to have predicted a bumper crop of olives one year, rented all of the olive presses in the region, and sublet them

full of heartbreak and disturbing emotions. See Gillian Clark, *Women in Late Antiquity: Pagan and Christian Life-Styles* (Oxford: Clarendon Press, 1993), 98–101.

38. Clark, *Women in Late Antiquity*, 100.

39. Clark (100) highlights the ready availability of these woven goods for sale in her discussion of John Chrysostom's treatise, *Against those men cohabiting with virgins*, 9, p. 47, 507.

at a profit later on in order to prove that philosophers could use their knowledge to make money, but chose not to.[40]

It is also likely that Sosipatra would have overseen family meals in some way or other, whether directly herself or by managing and directing staff. If she and Eustathius lived in an urban setting, some of their provisions would have come from their estate(s) and some would have been procured locally. The urban residences of wealthier individuals were used to conduct business activities and "were open not only to the family but also to clients, guests, and unannounced visitors."[41] Sosipatra would have had to ensure that all anticipated and unanticipated guests were accommodated according to the standards of what Eunapius called "Greek hospitality." Given our current North American culture in which "cookery" is an obsession of sorts for men and women of a wide range of social classes and backgrounds, we might be inclined to assume that elite homes in ancient urban settings would have boasted large kitchens in addition to comfortably luxurious dining rooms. But archaeological evidence suggests different patterns. Based on evidence from the third-century terrace houses at Ephesus, we can identify only two in house kitchens; "Otherwise, the utilitarian areas are centrally located and could be used by a number of houses at the same time."[42] With this model, "more than one family shared one tract for utilitarian purposes." In these spaces we find "not only areas of storage and preparation of food and drink but also storage and utility rooms as well as the *praefurnia* of connected bathing establishments."[43] This setup makes sense from an efficiency and fire safety perspective, combining ovens for baking and furnaces for heating baths along with what we might call kitchens and pantries for multiple households. It is unlikely that this sort of arrangement was unique to third-century Ephesus. It may have also been the norm in Pergamum and other cities in Asia Minor in Late Antiquity as well.

Additionally, in Ephesus, we find "incised receipts for delivered food on plaster walls," which indicates that residences may have also brought in food prepared by cook shops for guests and household members.

40. G. S. Kirk, J. E. Raven, and Malcolm Schofield, *The Presocratic Philosophers: A Critical History with a Selection of Texts*, 2nd ed. (Cambridge: Cambridge University Press, 1983), 80–81.

41. Helmut Schwaizer, "Domestic Architecture in Ephesus from the Hellenistic Period to Late Antiquity," in *Mediterranean Families in Antiquity: Households, Extended Families, and Domestic Space*, ed. Sabine R. Huebner and Geoffrey S Nathan (Chichester: Wiley Blackwell, 2017), 85.

42. Schwaizer, "Domestic Architecture in Ephesus," 86.

43. Schwaizer, "Domestic Architecture in Ephesus," 86.

Hence, "cooking in the family context, at least for the elites in Ephesus, must have played only a subsidiary role: more frequently cook shops were visited and ready-prepared food was brought home."[44] All of this would have still required management and coordination by Sosipatra or a trusted household staff member if family and guests were to be properly looked after.

Religious Household Management

In addition to the practical aspects of household management which Sosipatra was likely in charge of, she would have also been responsible, in cooperation and coordination with Eustathius, for tending to the well-being of the household by maintaining connections with various spirits and divinities at domestic and civic levels. Some of these activities would have happened on a daily basis, others monthly or annually, and others occasionally in the case of births, marriages, and deaths. Until his death or departure, Eustathius, as patriarch, would have been in charge of leading the traditional household cult, which likely involved daily offerings of incense, cakes, drinks, fruits, or grains to images of specific gods in some way important to the family, as well as to ancestral spirits. In Roman religion, the Lares and Penates were generalized spirits of the dead, represented in votive or figurine form on household shrines. It is possible that residents of the Roman East may have incorporated similar ideas and practices over time. Regardless, the family shrine would have been populated by representations of other divinities important to the household. When Eustathius died, depending on whether his role as patriarch devolved on a male relative, it may have been Sosipatra who took over care of the family shrine and rituals associated with it. She may have also been responsible for other more femininely coded household rituals associated with the hearth and pantry.

Traditionally in the classical Greek world, changes in the "membership of the family group," whether through birth, marriage, the acquisition of slaves, and so forth, were "recognized or articulated by rituals connected with the hearth" in which wives would have played significant roles.[45] Women's ritual roles in the home were also critical

44. Schwaizer, "Domestic Architecture in Ephesus," 86.

45. Janett Morgan, "Women, Religion, and the Home," in *A Companion to Greek Religion*, ed. Daniel Ogden (Maldon, MA: Wiley-Blackwell, 2007), 302. Although Janett Morgan focuses many

in mitigating pollution and peril associated with a range of transitions, in particular, the incorporation or loss of new members through birth, marriage, and especially death. In other words, women "become visible in our sources at religious sites that change the composition of the family."[46] These moments, in particular birth and death—and statistically these were one and the same with far more frequency than we are accustomed to today—were fraught and dangerous. The home and larger world could become perilous; as "the dead mix with the living, the future of the household is in jeopardy as the wife risks death in childbirth and the vulnerable bride, neither girl nor wife, walks the streets of the city."[47] Women's ritual activity in these circumstances "is concerned with restoring harmony; their actions remove the ritual pollution and danger associated with rites of transition. They heal both family and community.[48]

In the case of the births of Sosipatra's sons and the death of her husband or other household members, for instance, she would have borne the responsibility for overseeing the necessary rituals within the home to remove pollution and to signal to the community through various markers on the house what was happening inside as a kind of warning. In the case of births, the sex of the child may even have been announced by hanging different materials on the outside of the door.

In ancient Athens, a pot of water was placed at the entry to a house where a recent death had occurred. In this situation, "precautions might include providing lustral water to help purify those who came in contact with the house, avoiding sacrifices to household or civic gods, and refraining from eating and bathing until after the body was carried out of the house."[49] Who knows what kinds of signs or markers would have been used in mid-fourth-century Asia Minor when someone died. They may have been particular to specific regions or cities. But we can assume that non-Christian, non-Jewish polytheists would have continued to mark major life transitions through rituals that bore some meaning,

of her observations on this topic on classical Athens, there is little reason to question the likelihood of continuity in the matter of women's roles in this kind of mitigation and management of pollution.

46. Morgan, "Women, Religion, and the Home," 306.
47. Morgan, "Women, Religion, and the Home," 306.
48. Morgan, "Women, Religion, and the Home," 306.
49. Deborah Boedeker, "Family Matters: Domestic Religion in Classical Greece," in *Household and Family Religion in Antiquity*, ed. John Bodel and Saul M. Olyan (Malden, MA: Wiley-Blackwell, 2009), 240–41.

much like nominal Christians today continue to christen their babies or recite Psalms at gravesides, and insist on the ritual involvement of church-sanctioned ministers in these life altering moments.

Sosipatra would have also been responsible for meeting the needs of the household dead in the context of the traditional funerary cult, which involved arrangements for feasting with and feeding the spirits of the dead at their tombs at particular times of the year. And we know that women's involvement in death rituals was slow to change in Late Antiquity even with Christianization.[50]

We might ask, however, about Sosipatra in particular and whether she would have participated in these rituals of transition. Or might we assume that because she was a philosopher of the highest order, according to Eunapius, she would have eschewed these forms of ritual engagement and participation as so much "superstitious nonsense"? Given what we know about the particular lineage she inhabits as constructed by Eunapius, I would argue that this would be a mistaken assumption. Instead, it would be in keeping with Eunapius's narrative that she would have also observed these kinds of ritual traditions. Theurgic philosophy in the Iamblichan lineage understood traditional ritual as part of a cosmic system created by the demiurge and the celestial gods for enabling all humans to participate in salvation, that is, purification and divinization of the soul. Within that context, we can imagine that Sosipatra would have understood participation in household and civic ritual—and even elective cults—as in keeping with her role as a theurgic philosopher. Who better to conduct such rituals than one in possession of a complete understanding of the mechanisms of the cosmos for remedying imbalance and disharmony of the soul in a sublunary context.

As a respectable elite citizen, it is also likely that Sosipatra would have participated in the civic cult of whichever city she lived in whether Ephesus (in her youth) or Pergamum (as a widow and teacher). We already discussed the possibility that she may have joined in processions for Artemis of Ephesus as a girl. However, ascertaining more precisely what Sosipatra's normal religious and ritual activities might have been is difficult for a number of reasons. We have very little information about specific late ancient urban religious calendars, nor do we have

50. Sharon Lorraine Murphy-Morgan, "Women and Death Rituals in Late Antiquity: Forming the Christian Identity" (Master's Thesis, University of Calgary, 2011).

FIGURE 3.2 Statue of Julia Domna, wife of Emperor Septimius Severus (193–211 CE), as a Priestess of Isis, marble, 207–209 CE. Louvre Museum. Courtesy of the author. Photo by author.

much in terms of sources for elite attitudes toward and levels of participation in the civic cult. If we look later in the fourth century around the time of Eunapius's flourishing, to the works of someone such as Libanius, we see dismay expressed at the lack of engagement in traditional worship in Antioch during his time. And Eunapius certainly expresses discouragement about the threatened nature of traditional cults in his day. But Sosipatra was of an earlier generation when Greco-Roman, Egyptian, and other "ethnically coded" cults continued free from the violent forms of opposition and intervention that we see later in the century. On the basis of mid-fourth-century calendars and literary sources. it seems that the traditional festivals of the Greek cities of the Imperial East "were still a vital part of civic life."[51] Certainly in the Imperial epoch, we have evidence that there was a "heightened splendor of processions" and "ampleness of food and drink," and largesse by civic benefactors in hosting and funding festivals was common.[52] Some of this may have changed in the third century due to political and economic upheaval. But the mid-fourth century was likely more stable. The point is that there is no reason to think that the urban context in which Sosipatra lived did not have a robust traditional and civic ritual program in which she could have participated. And as an upstanding citizen wife, she likely saw this participation as an important duty.

Childbirth and Childrearing

If Eunapius is to be believed, Sosipatra gave birth to three sons in five or so years, possibly at as young an age as her mid to late teens. More likely this happened in her late teens and early twenties. Given the statistical realities of miscarriage, stillbirths, and high infant mortality, she would have been extraordinarily fortunate if these were her only three pregnancies. Some scholars estimate that infant and child mortality rates for the ancient world were as high as one third of all births. Many of these children would have died at birth or shortly thereafter.[53] So statistically, it is unlikely that Sosipatra would have given birth only three

51. Graf, *Roman Festivals in the Greek East*, 59.
52. Graf, *Roman Festivals*, 59.
53. Maria Doerfler, "Holy Households," in *Melania: Early Christianity through the Life of One Family*, ed. C. M. Chin and Caroline T. Schroeder (Berkeley: University of California Press, 2016), 72.

times, and it was unusual that her three sons all survived childhood and grew to be adults, which it seems they did. Sosipatra's life in pregnancy and childbirth was also in acute danger. But both Sosipatra and her three sons were extraordinarily lucky, even if Eustathius was not. They beat the ancient odds, so to speak. Attitudes toward the deaths of infants and young children varied in antiquity depending on where one looks, whether it be the moving epitaphs mourning the loss of children, Stoic exhortations to maintain equanimity in the face of such tragedy, or other sources that reflect sentiments that strike modern readers as more callous.

When each of her sons was born, he would have been carefully examined by the midwife in order to determine if he was worth rearing. If the child was accepted as such, the midwife would then have cut the umbilical cord and given him his first bath.[54] This would have had symbolic significance in separating the infant from uterine life and introducing "the child to earthly existence through contact with elements, such as water."[55] To celebrate the birth of her sons, a household member would have hung an olive wreath or some other sort of symbol on the outside of the house to signal the happy occasion. As in the case of the infant Sosipatra, the boys would have been massaged, swaddled, and breastfed.[56] And on the ninth day, they would have received their names.[57] The family may have also performed some sort of ceremony, possibly around the hearth or household altar, to incorporate each child into the family once named.

Sosipatra as Mother

We might ask how Sosipatra, a wealthy, elite woman, with a relatively large household staff, might have cared for her infant boys. For answers to this question, we can turn to a number of different kinds of sources— for instance, literary texts, medical writings, and moral works in the form of treatises and letters. Unfortunately, on specific questions such as

54. Véronique Dasen, "Childbirth and Infancy in Greek and Roman Antiquity," in *A Companion to Families in the Greek and Roman Worlds*, ed. Beryl Rawson, Blackwell Companions to the Ancient World. Literature and Culture (Malden, MA: Wiley-Blackwell, 2011), 297–300.

55. Dasen, "Childbirth and Infancy," 300.

56. Dasen, "Childbirth and Infancy," 302–3.

57. Dasen, "Childbirth and Infancy," 303–4.

whether a mother should breastfeed her own children or hand the task over to a wet nurse, we find a variety of opinions expressed across our sources. But we can sketch a general view based on a number of points of agreement in these sources. Many texts exhort women to breastfeed their own children. The reasons given for breastfeeding one's own children are unlike our own "attachment theory"-based reasons, namely, early bonding and trust between mother and child. Rather, the ancient reasons are based on medico-philosophical ideas about milk as a substance that not only provides sustenance and nutrition for the child but also conveys the mother's good character to the infant: "In the Roman Empire, growth in virtue and wisdom was the result of proper feeding." On this view, women's bodies were "imbued with a significant power to transmit the 'stuff' of cultural or familial identity to a child."[58]

We see some of these assumptions about breastfeeding as part of proper human formation and stable social order expressed in an anecdote about Favorinus, the Sophist, found in Aelus Gellius's *Attic Nights*. In this passage, Favorinus rebukes an elite woman for handing her infant over to a wet nurse. In doing so, the Sophist "draws upon the well-attested ancient medical tradition that viewed maternal milk as blood frothed up by the heat of the mother's post-partem body." On this view, "the essential material contained in breast milk . . . is just as potent as the father's seed in the transmission of both physical and intellectual characteristics."[59] In other words, "breastfeeding is thus understood here as a powerful transfer of elemental essences that have a transformative effect upon the child's entire nature and establishes its bonds of kinship, physical vitality, and intellectual capacities."[60] We can connect this view with a more general understanding found in Galen's *The Soul's Dependence on the Body* of how dietetic regimen could affect moral character and intellectual capacity.

This view of mother's milk as transmitting values and character also mirrors embryological theories asserting that a mother needed to have beautiful images before her when conceiving and during pregnancy because her faculty of imagination (*phantasia*) could in turn imprint these images on the child's form. This is a view that Porphyry, one of

58. John David Penniman, "Fed to Perfection: Mother's Milk, Roman Family Values, and the Transformation of the Soul in Gregory of Nyssa," *Church History* 84, no. 3 (2015): 497.
59. Penniman, "Fed to Perfection," 500.
60. Penniman, "Fed to Perfection," 500.

Iamblichus's predecessors and teachers, advanced in his work *To Gaurus on the Ensoulment of Embryos*.[61] So Sosipatra may have also paid careful attention to what she was exposed to, what she imagined, and what she consumed during her pregnancy. Given her level of education, her position in a lineage that went back to Iamblichus and through him to Porphyry, and the association we know of between Eunapius and the medical writer, Oribasius, who was himself an adherent of Galenic medicine and an expert on regimen, it would be safe for us to assume that Sosipatra would have taken care of her sons to ensure optimal conditions for their physical and moral development right from the beginnings of their lives.

Despite the objections of Favorinus to the use of wet nurses, many mothers did hand their children over to these women for nurturing and care. If Sosipatra did this, she would have paid careful attention to her choice of wet nurse. This woman would likely have spoken Greek as her first language. An attractive woman was also desirable because the child's mind was like wax and should be molded by attending to beauty.[62] She would have also had to follow a strict dietary and behavioral regimen, abstaining, in particular, from sexual activity lest she become pregnant and additional, unforeseen influence enter the nutritional and formative equation in the form of a different father's sperm.[63] In medical literature, we even find instances where wet nurses would participate in treating a sick infant by following a regimen for a particular disease themselves such that the milk produced under these circumstances—including special diet, baths, massages, and various drugs—would become medicine for the infant's condition.[64] Sosipatra's sons may have become very close to their wet nurses if they had them. Some children had life-long relationships with these caregivers, sometimes granting them their freedom or leaving bequests to them in their wills. These caregivers and others under Sosipatra's direction, and perhaps with her participation, would have also engaged in other methods of forming the infant who was understood as a kind of "imperfect, weak, ugly, malleable," unformed, wax-like, deficient being barely more than a vegetable.[65] They would have

---

61. James Wilberding, *Porphyry: To Gaurus on How Embryos Are Ensouled and On What Is in Our Power* (Bristol: Bristol Classical Press, 2011).

62. Dasen, "Childbirth and Infancy," 308.

63. Dasen, "Childbirth and Infancy," 308.

64. Dasen, "Childbirth and Infancy," 295.

65. Dasen, "Childbirth and Infancy," 293.

massaged the child to encourage a fine form and swaddled it for the same reasons.[66]

We might ask if Sosipatra would have comforted and held her children if they cried. Once again, we can't know, but we do find a recommendation in Plato's *Laws* that crying infants ought to be cuddled as opposed to Aristotle who argued that crying was a form of exercise.[67] It would be comforting to think that Sosipatra might have followed the Platonist line on this matter.

Sosipatra as Widow and/or Single Mother

As we know from Sosipatra's own upbringing, the education of her boys would have started quite young at home. By five years of age, they were likely all in some sort of educational program with tutors, or they may have been taught by Sosipatra herself. In any case, she would have been in charge of their early education, and when Eustathius died or departed, she likely continued in this role as they grew up.

Before we can talk more about the ways in which she might have raised her three sons in late ancient Asia Minor, we need to discuss more generally the ways in which being separated or widowed at a relatively young age with three small children may have changed her life. Eunapius provides us with a few biographical details on this moment in her life:

> Sosipatra, after Eustathius passed away, returned to her former properties and was passing her time in Asia and ancient Pergamum. The great Aedesius treated her with affection, provided for her, and he was educating her sons.[68]

To begin, we need to discuss the possibility that Eustathius left Sosipatra and did not in fact die. The Greek word *apochóresin* can mean either "departure" or "death."[69] Garth Fowden and Robert J. Penella both argue that it is more likely that Eunapius meant the former. They argue this on the basis of a chronological confusion in Eunapius's account.[70] The

---

66. Dasen, "Childbirth and Infancy," 293.

67. Dasen, "Childbirth and Infancy," 293.

68. Eunap., *VS* 6.80.

69. Robert J. Penella, *Greek Philosophers and Sophists in the Fourth Century A.D.: Studies in Eunapius of Sardis* (Leeds: Francis Cairns, 1990), 54.

70. Penella, *Greek Philosophers and Sophists,* 53–56.

confusion emerges when we compare Eunapius's description of the timeline of Sosipatra's marriage and Eustathius's death after five years with his description of Eustathius's career as an imperial ambassador to Persia. Hence either Eunapius has some of his facts wrong or he purposely introduces ambiguity into his account in order to avoid disclosing the dissolution of the marriage and to preserve the image of marital concord. The important point, for our purposes, is that Sosipatra was left on her own to raise her children "as early as the end of the 330's."[71] Her son, Antoninus, would have been anywhere between eight and twenty years old, "hence still a *pais*" or child.

Despite being uncertain about whether Sosipatra was separated or widowed, there is, nonetheless, a lot we can draw out from Eunapius's description of the moment when Sosipatra becomes responsible for her sons. There is also a great deal about which we can only speculate. For instance, we do not know where Sosipatra returned from. But it is likely to have been from Aedesius's estate in Cappadocia, which Eustathius may still have been managing for his kinsman while married. On the other hand, it could have been from Eustathius's own family estate to which Sosipatra and her sons had no claim upon his departure or death because of other inheritance arrangements. In the case of his death, Eustathius may not have had any male relatives who could serve as a guardian for Sosipatra's sons. Alternately, she may have chosen to act as their guardians herself, or Aedesius may have taken on this role, which is why she and her sons moved near him. In other words, the relationship with Aedesius described by Eunapius may have been a formal one of legal guardianship. It is impossible to determine how extensive her property holdings were. We do not, however, get a sense from the narrative that the relationship between Aedesius and Sosipatra was itself conjugal. She may have only had an urban house in Pergamum, but this is unlikely given the wealth her father seems to have possessed. It is also unlikely that no other property was left to her sons by their father upon his death.

Hence, all kinds of situations may have been the case. First, Sosipatra may have had multiple properties from her family if she were the only child of her parents. Some of these or all may have been part of her dowry and hence came back to her upon Eustathius's death. She then

71. Penella, *Greek Philosophers and Sophists,* 53.

managed them in trust for her sons. Or she may have had property, which was part of Eustathius's bridal gift to her, which she managed in trust for her sons. Sosipatra may have chosen to hand over management of her properties in either of the foregoing scenarios to Aedesius as a guardian. As he was a kinsman of Eustathius, this would have been an appropriate arrangement. And he would have thereby provided for her maintenance and that of her sons from the resources generated by her properties. However, it is unlikely that she was dependent on him due to a lack of funds. Such guardianship arrangements would have been her choice. Given the fact that she had three sons, didn't remarry, and was a woman of means and a certain social class and intelligence, she could have served as her sons' legal guardian herself.

It is important to remember, in this regard, that in the fourth century, and even earlier, the social and legal status of widows was changing quite profoundly. This was, in part, the result of the impact of changing religious realities in the Roman Empire. The expanding Christian Church did much to institutionalize the status of widows, in part, to keep them in a certain place and in certain roles (out of the "pulpit" and baptismal font, we might say), and to administer both their poverty and their wealth. Traditionally, based on Augustan legislation, propertied women who were widowed, especially at a younger age, were expected to remarry and were penalized for not doing so. Constantine abolished these laws, allowing widows to remain unmarried.

As they grew up, Sosipatra would have continued to make decisions about her sons' education. In her nuptial prophecy, Sosipatra foretold that all three sons would achieve success in a worldly or human sense. But only one, Antoninus, would achieve success in a divine register. In the case of her less inspired sons, we can imagine that they would have gone through the standard grammatical and rhetorical training of the time and then perhaps received additional training that prepared them to take on military or administrative positions, or possibly both. Indeed, a mother's importance in her son's life did not decline as the boy approached adolescence. Rather, "the respect accorded the mother by her adolescent or adult son appears to have been strengthened by the general social esteem in which a Roman matron was held and her association as partner rather than obvious subordinate in parental activities."[72] This authority was only enhanced by widowhood. And in general,

72. Suzanne Dixon, *The Roman Mother* (Norman: University of Oklahoma Press, 1988), 176.

women's ambitions tended to be focused more on their sons than on their husbands.[73] Furthermore, a widowed *materfamilias* could exercise discretion over her children's lives and manage property on their behalf without concern for interference and exploitation by her husband's male relatives.[74] It is important to note that some of these trends that favored maternal control over male children were crystallizing during Sosipatra's lifetime.

In the case of her two more worldly sons, Sosipatra likely also helped to arrange advantageous marriages with young women from good families who "were already connected by blood or affinal alliance."[75] Sosipatra would have been obliged to make good betrothal arrangements for her sons, because the interests of both the state and the family were at stake:

> Since the main purpose of marriage was the transmission of
> family name and property to the next generation and thereby
> the continuation not only of individual family lines but of
> the Roman state itself, rules were needed to ensure that the
> allying of families and the passing on of property were done
> properly.[76]

There is no reason to think that Sosipatra, in alliance and consultation with Aedesius, if he lived long enough to still be of assistance in these arrangements, would not have done everything properly in this respect. If we are looking for an example of a widow in a similar position to Sosipatra but from a slightly later period and slightly lower socioeconomic status, we can think of Monica, Augustine's mother, and the arrangements she made for him vis-à-vis his education, career, and marriage prospects.

Eunapius describes Sosipatra's son Antoninus as having achieved a different measure of success, one considered noble for the gods. By this Eunapius means that he followed more closely in his mother's footsteps and studied divine philosophy, eschewing more standard career paths for men of his class. His preparation for this type of success would

---

73. Dixon, *The Roman Mother*, 203.

74. Geoffrey S. Nathan, *The Family in Late Antiquity: The Rise of Christianity and the Endurance of Tradition* (London: Routledge, 2000), 84.

75. Evans Grubbs, *Law and Family in Late Antiquity*, 153.

76. Evans Grubbs, *Law and Family in Late* Antiquity, 140.

have involved additional education in philosophy, not just the standard training in grammar and rhetoric. And Eunapius also implies that his preparation involved some form of initiation into Egyptian mysteries. He writes that Antoninus "dwelled at the Canobic mouth of the Nile and having dedicated himself wholly to the hallowed things there, he spent his strength on the prophesies of his mother."[77] He became a teacher of sorts in the temple to "young men who had healthy souls and had set their hearts on philosophy."[78] This educational program blending traditional philosophy with initiations and sacred mysteries, this time Egyptian, is not unfamiliar to us, as we discussed a similar sort of hybrid education between philosophy and Chaldean theurgy in the case of Sosipatra in Chapter 3. We will also consider the nature of philosophical education in Late Antiquity in more detail in Chapter 4 when we discuss what Sosipatra and Aedesius may have taught in their respective schools. But we might wonder why Antoninus chose to focus his theurgical or ritual/theological program on Egyptian cults rather than on the Chaldean mysteries into which his mother was initiated. If we look back through the Eunapian philosophical lineage to Iamblichus, we see that this fascination with Egyptian worship is nothing new. Iamblichus wrote *On the Mysteries of Egypt* in the guise of an Egyptian priest, Abamon. Before him, we can point to Plutarch, who offered Platonist readings and interpretations of Egyptian myths. And as already mentioned, many middle and late Platonists thought of philosophy in its truest, most divine form as a distillation of all the most ancient wisdom traditions whether Chaldean, Egyptian, Hebrew, Greek, or others. In Chapter 6 we will discuss the specifically theurgical or ritual focus of late Platonism as reflected in Eunapius's telling of Sosipatra's story and discuss how this framework also explains Antoninus's choice to spend part of his life in a temple of Serapis.

77. Eunap., *VS* 6.95.
78. Eunap., *VS* 6.95.

4

Sosipatra as a Teacher

After Eustathius died or departed from his family, as we discovered in Chapter 3, Sosipatra chose to move to Pergamum, perhaps from Cappadocia where her husband had been managing Aedesius's estate. Pergamum was near her own estate, perhaps the one on which she was educated by Chaldeans near Ephesus. She handed over its management to Aedesius and opened up a philosophy school in her home in the city. As we know, elites of Sosipatra's class often had multiple residences, some in the cities and some in the country.

Furthermore, Eunapius relates that she competed with Aedesius as she philosophized in her own house. Students, after attending his lectures, would go to hear hers.[1] It was likely a friendly competition, if it was a competition at all. The rivalries we hear about between teachers and schools in other large urban settings such as Athens were far less friendly. Eunapius compares their teaching styles thus: "and there was no one who did not greatly love and admire the accuracy of Aedisius in what he said, and did not adore and revere the divine inspiration of the woman."[2]

What did she teach, we might ask, that was so inspiring of adoration and reverence? Eunapius does not really tell us except in the course of relating an episode of remote viewing wherein she observes her kinsman Philometer's carriage accident. Just prior to this moment of revelation, she was teaching on the nature of the soul, on its descent, "and about what is punished and what immortal."[3]

1. Eunap., *VS* 6.81.
2. Eunap., *VS* 6.81.
3. Eunap., *VS* 6.91.

As with all the foregoing chapters and their themes, Eunapius provides us a few tantalizing details, glimpses here and there, of Sosipatra's life, this time as a philosophy teacher. And we must do our best, once again, to take these details and weave them into some sort of more complete and contextualized picture. In order to do so, we will need to answer a number of questions. How did philosophy schools function in Late Antiquity? What would the setting have been like for Sosipatra's home school? How might her gender have factored into the setting? What did philosophical education in the Neo-Pythagorean, late Platonic lineage of Iamblichus look like in terms of curriculum in the fourth century? In other words, what might Aedesius or Sosipatra have taught in their schools? What might students have learned at Aedesius's school versus at Sosipatra's? What is Eunapius trying to signal by marking the difference between their teachings? What other images of philosophy schools, whether actual or ideal, do we have to compare Sosipatra's school with from roughly the same period? What other female philosophy teachers do we know of with whom we can compare Sosipatra and her teaching activities?

The Setting and Structure of Philosophical Education in Late Antiquity

As we know from Chapter 3, schooling in philosophy was one of the highest forms of education available to those wealthy enough to afford it in Late Antiquity. It was one of the three main areas of specialization, the other two being legal and medical training; it followed after young men, and sometimes young women, had spent time in a school of grammar and then rhetoric.[4] Although "in classical Greece philosophical life was dominated by the great schools founded in the fourth and early third centuries," such as Plato's Academy, Theophrastus's Lyceum (devoted to Peripatetic philosophy), and the school of Epicurus, in the fourth century CE, the situation was significantly different.[5] Philosophical education was more diverse, hybrid, and diffuse. Schools were organized around individual teachers, many of whom taught unique syntheses of

---

4. Edward Jay Watts, "Education: Speaking, Thinking and Socializing," in *Oxford Handbook of Late Antiquity*, ed. Scott Fitzgerald Johnson (Oxford: Oxford University Press, 2012), 469–70.

5. Garth Fowden, "The Platonist Philosopher and His Circle in Late Antiquity," *Philosophia* 7 (1977): 359.

authoritative texts and teachings from figures such as the Pre-Socratics philosophers, including Pythagoras, Plato, and Aristotle and their successors, including the "Middle Platonists." In this respect, it is difficult to talk about a school of Iamblichus, much less a school of Sosipatra if we mean by that something like Plato's Academy. Rather, it is better to speak of a lineage, and in the case of the lineage in which Sosipatra teaches, we already know that it was as much a construction of Eunapius as it was an independently existing lineage.

A late ancient philosophy school in the Platonist tradition was, in essence, "a group of students living in or around their teacher, meeting with him daily, and probably dining with him, pursuing a set course of reading and study in the works of Aristotle and Plato and holding disputations on set topics."[6] These kinds of late Platonist schools were defined by a few key features. First, their main goal "was not the preservation of an inherited dogma" but the "desire to associate with and learn from a specific individual teacher whose disciples tended not to maintain group identity after his death."[7] That being said, texts such as Eunapius's *Lives* and Porphyry's *Life of Plotinus* provide some evidence that the authors of these works, at least, were certainly engaged in creating group identities and unambiguous lineages for their own purposes. But they did so for audiences who were receptive to their interpretations of events. Additionally, these group identities were often maintained through oral testimonies, which likely served as the basis for written narratives where we have them.[8] Part of this oral testimony are stories about the relationships between legendary teachers and their students who go on to become teachers themselves following clear, albeit in some cases fictional, lines of succession. And there is sometimes evidence in these narratives, if one reads carefully, of competition between members of a teacher's inner group for succession.

For instance, in the *Life of Plotinus*, Erennius, Origen, and Plotinus were all students of Ammonius Saccas who made a pact among themselves not to reveal his most important teachings. Porphyry accused Erennius and Origen of betraying this pact.[9] He also describes an episode

---

6. John Dillon and Jackson P. Hershbell, *Iamblichus: On the Pythagorean Way of Life*, Society of Biblical Literature, Texts and Translations 29 (Atlanta, GA: Scholars Press, 1991), 21.

7. Fowden, "The Platonist Philosopher," 379.

8. Edward Jay Watts, "Orality and Communal Identity in Eunapius' Lives of the Sophists and Philosophers," *Byzantion*, no. 75 (2005): 334–61.

9. Porph., *Plot.* 3.

where Origen showed up unexpectedly at one of Plotinus's lectures in Rome filling him with embarrassment.[10] Porphyry doesn't tell us why Plotinus blushed, but perhaps it was because he was caught teaching the wisdom of Ammonius Saccas himself, indicating that he saw himself as the true successor in their teacher's lineage. Porphyry also seems to have been in competition with other students of Plotinus over who was next in line. He edited Plotinus's lectures, in other words, the *Enneads*. And he wrote a biographical account of his teacher. Both served to establish him as a Plotinian expert. But it seems that Amelius was also involved in editing Plotinus's lectures or at least in compiling notebooks for his teacher prior to Porphyry's arrival at the school.[11]

An additional feature of late ancient philosophy schools relates to the status of the teachers themselves. These individuals were often thought of as "holy men as much as philosophers and their followers were inspired as much by personal devotion as by desire for intellectual instruction."[12] Sosipatra certainly fits this description as her educational pedigree and virtuosity signal some sort of divine inspiration as the source of her knowledge and wisdom.[13]

A further feature of late ancient philosophy schools is the tendency for disciples to be divided between "an inner group of close associates and a larger body of pupils."[14] This larger body was frequently instructed by the inner circle of students. Finally, some of these close circles "seem to have enjoyed a common life, their sense of community fostered by a shared but not rigorous asceticism."[15]

When it comes to the shared schools of Aedesius and Sosipatra, one wonders if Aedesius was responsible for teaching the larger group of pupils and Sosipatra dealt mainly with what Fowden calls the "inner circle." This is possible given what Eunapius says about the nature of her teaching, namely, its inspired quality. That being said, however, other statements—for instance, those about her ability to recite, understand, and interpret perfectly the works of poets, rhetoricians, and philosophers after her early educational experiences with her Chaldean

---

10. Porph., *Plot.* 14.

11. Porph., *Plot.* 4.

12. Fowden, "The Platonist Philosopher," 361.

13. Ilinca Tanaseanu-Döbler, "Religious Education in Late Antique Paganism," in *Religious Education in Pre-Modern Europe*, ed. Ilinca Tanaseanu-Döbler and Marvin Döbler (Leiden: Brill, 2012), 133.

14. Fowden, "The Platonist Philosopher," 379.

15. Fowden, "The Platonist Philosopher," 379.

teachers—implies that she would have been capable of offering instruction on a full range of texts and topics.

Although the key features of late ancient philosophy schools work well to explain certain aspects of Aedesius's and Sosipatra's schools, the two of them seem to have avoided another feature—the more unfriendly and at times violent competition between schools and their students. For instance, we know of one contemporary incident in Athens when the "*choroi*" or inner circle of two professors, Julianus and Apsines engaged in a "street battle" that was so disruptive that "when a complaint about the violence was filed by students of Apsines, the proconsul of Achaea ordered the arrest" of Julianus and his entire school: "The idea behind this collective punishment seems to be that the school as a whole shared responsibility for the violence, because it had been motivated by the interests of the *choros* and the professor it served."[16]

These expressions of loyalty to a teacher were part and parcel of the kind of commitment students were expected to make to their teacher and fellow students. This loyalty was inculcated through initiation rituals, the language of familial relationships, and close personal intimacy.[17] Some initiation rituals were themselves rather violent, involving kidnapping of prospective students fresh off the boat, so to speak, by loyal pupils (the *chorus* mentioned above) of a specific teacher. One initiation rite seems to have involved marching new students in procession to the baths, pushing, pulling, and jostling them along the way, where they would be undressed and scrubbed roughly, and eventually given the right to wear the tribon indicating their status as students.[18] Whether any of this was standard operating procedure in a place such as Pergamum in the time of Sosipatra or whether it was particular to the philosophy schools in Athens, one can imagine that students of Aedesius and Sosipatra were more likely to have seen the two teachers as complimentary and cooperative partners, philosophical parents of a sort, rather than as rivals or competitors, especially given the close familial connections between the two. And they likely felt strong loyalty to both of them.

16. Edward Jay Watts, "The Student Self in Late Antiquity," in *Religion and the Self in Antiquity*, ed. David Brakke, Michale L. Satlow, and Steven Weitzman (Bloomington: Indiana University Press, 2005), 240. This episode takes place at Eunap., *VS* 483 (Loeb edition).

17. Watts, "The Student Self in Late Antiquity," 240.

18. Watts, "The Student Self in Late Antiquity," 238. Here Watts references Fragment 28 from Olympiodorus.

Furthermore, based on Eunapius's tendency to create ideal images of his favorite subjects, such as Sosipatra or Chrysanthius, it is important to also consider what kinds of more complimentary or positive depictions of philosophical schools were in circulation at the time to inspire his subjects as well as himself. The most compelling depiction of this sort is one produced by Iamblichus in his *On the Pythagorean Life* mentioned earlier. In this work, Iamblichus provides a detailed description of his understanding of the ideal philosophical life, wherein Pythagoras not only teaches his students philosophy but also provides comprehensive guidance on their entire lives. This included advice on what to eat, how often his students ought to frequent temples, what materials they should wear and use as bed linens, and so forth. These latter details are important to Iamblichus because certain textiles, foods, sounds, times of day, and so forth had sacred and cosmic significance. Furthermore, Pythagoras is depicted as healing sick pupils by playing music for them, just one example of his polymathic understanding of the cosmos that allowed him to tend to the total care of his students.[19] It is a comprehensive, totalizing program for the care of psyche and soma that includes critical ritual elements. It is a romantic, idealized picture, but one that Iamblichus likely crafted to authorize his own vision of philosophical education.[20]

Gender and Sosipatra's School

Trying to assess whether it was problematic for a woman to lead a philosophy school in Late Antiquity and the role gender may have played in the school's location, curriculum, student body, and so forth, is a difficult task. Christian women were certainly prohibited from teaching men. But the examples of women such as Sosipatra and Hypatia seem to indicate that many non-Christian men and women found it perfectly acceptable for an elite woman to choose this vocation. Given the cost of education, especially at the higher levels, it is not surprising that the only women who were able to do this came from wealthy families. Some

---

19. Iamb., *Vita Pyth.* 25.110–11.

20. Heidi Marx-Wolf, "Pythagoras the Theurgist: Porphyry and Iamblichus on the Role of Ritual in the Philosophical Life," in *Religious Competition in the Third Century CE: Jews, Christians, and the Greco-Roman World*, ed. Jordan Rosenblum, Lily Vuong, and Nathaniel DesRosiers (Göttingen: Vandenhoeck & Ruprecht, 2014), 32–38.

scholars have pointed to Sosipatra's teaching in her own home as an indication that she felt the need to circumvent the obstacles presented by her gender by remaining in a domestic space.[21] Others have seen it as a way of avoiding detection for "pagan" women engaged in teaching and practicing more esoteric forms of Platonism.[22] But Aedesius and many other men also taught in their own homes. This was a common practice throughout antiquity.

In general, in the Platonist and Neo-Pythagorean traditions in which Eunapius is embedded, we find relatively frequent mention of women who, even if they did not teach, led philosophical lives and learned from their fathers or husbands. Iamblichus goes so far as to include a list of seventeen famous Pythagorean women at the end of his *On the Pythagorean Way of Life*. Hence, I would argue that it is not until Christian mores governing gender roles became normative and enforceable (likely starting in the late fourth or early fifth century CE) that we see clearer prohibitions of women teaching in philosophical schools.

Curriculum in the Iamblichan Lineage

Eunapius doesn't tell us much about what was taught in the Platonic lineage in which he embeds Sosipatra, which means we have to look beyond his works to establish potential content. Iamblichus's philosophical program was a unique and fascinating synthesis of Platonic and Aristotelian thought influenced strongly by the addition of Neo-Pythagoreanism, via his reading of the second-century Middle Platonist Numenius. The latter taught in Apamea, the place where Iamblichus likely set up his own school after having studied with Porphyry of Tyre, perhaps in Rome in the late third century. Prior to this, Iamblichus studied with a certain Anatolius. This may have been the same Anatolius who was a teacher of Peripatetic philosophy in Alexandria in the 260s and later became bishop of Laodicea.[23] It may have been as a result of spending time

21. Arthur P. Urbano, *The Philosophical Life: Biography and the Crafting of Intellectual Identity in Late Antiquity*, Patristic Monograph Series, vol. 21 (Washington, DC: Catholic University of America Press, 2013), 266.

22. Nicola Denzey Lewis, "Living Images of the Divine; Female Theurgists in Late Antiquity," in *Daughters of Hecate: Women and Magic in the Ancient World*, ed. Dayna S. Kalleres and Kimberly B. Stratton (Oxford: Oxford University Press, 2014).

23. The best account of Iamblichus's life can be found in John Dillon, "Iamblichus of Chalcis (c. 240–325 AD)," *Aufstieg Und Niedergang Der Römischen Welt* 2, no. 36.2 (1987): 862–909. For a discussion of whether Anatolius was both teacher and bishop, see Elizabeth DePalma Digeser,

with Porphyry that Iamblichus expanded his intellectual and exegetical interests beyond traditional and canonical texts of philosophy to myths and poetry, such as Homer, oracles, including the Chaldaean oracles, prophecy, and ritual. All of these sources were considered to be divinely inspired and instituted and thereby sources of wisdom for students of philosophy in the theurgical intellectual tradition. Before we turn to a discussion of the pinnacle of philosophical education in the Iamblichan lineage, namely, theurgic philosophy, however, we should discuss the more rudimentary levels of philosophical training that may have been on offer in the schools of Aedesius and Sosipatra.

Iamblichus wrote ten volumes on Pythagoreanism, which probably "constituted an introductory course for his school."[24] The first volume was the work translated as *On the Pythagorean Way of Life*, a work that paints a vivid and colorful picture of Pythagoras's life, records many of his most famous sayings, and offers interpretations of some of these. It also gives a detailed account of his activities as a pedagogue and describes the activities of some of his followers. This work also presents readers with ideal images of philosophical circles, images that may have informed Eunapius's account of Sosipatra's school. In addition to this Pythagorean primer of sorts, students in Iamblichus's school would have studied "at least some Aristotle, the logical works, . . . the *De Anima*, and perhaps parts of the *Metaphysics*, followed by the study of Plato."[25] When it came to teaching Plato, Iamblichus likely followed "Middle Platonic systems of instruction" such as that outlined in Albinus's *Isagoge*.[26] In a work referred to as the *Anonymous Prologomena to Platonic Philosophy*, we find a discussion of an ordered course of ten Platonic dialogues attributed to Iamblichus. Students would start with *Alcibiades I*, then continue with *Gorgias, Phaedo, Cratylus, Theatetus, Sophist, Statesman, Phaedrus, Symposium*, and *Philebus*. They would end this course of learning with the *Timaeus* and the *Parmenides*.[27] It is interesting that neither Plato's *Republic* nor the *Laws* were part of this curriculum. This may have been because these works were too long, perhaps given the tendency in the classroom to work through texts line by line, the teacher

---

A Threat to Public Piety: Christians, Platonists, and the Great Persecution (Ithaca, NY: Cornell University Press, 2012), 109, ft. 61.

24. Dillon and Hershbell, *Iamblichus*, 21.
25. Dillon and Hershbell, *Iamblichus*, 21–22.
26. Dillon and Hershbell, *Iamblichus*, 22.
27. Dillon and Hershbell, *Iamblichus*, 22.

providing commentary as he or she proceeded. But there is evidence that sections of both these works "received due attention," sections such as *Republic* VI, VII, and X and *Laws* X.[28] In fact, as we will see, Sosipatra may have been lecturing on Book X of the *Republic*, and Plato's Myth of Er in particular, when she was interrupted by the vision of Philometer's carriage accident.[29] Many teachers would have proceeded to cover these authoritative works by way of a rather banal line-by-line discussion of the text and its meaning.[30] In other words, much time in the lecture room would have been taken up with formal exegesis.

The order of these texts by Plato seems to have mapped onto a graduated understanding of virtues that was developing among philosophers in the Plotinian lineage. Porphyry and Iamblichus were actively engaged in this conversation about virtues, each contributing additional layers of complexity to their hierarchical ordering. As a result, one of the ways in which we should be thinking about late ancient schools of philosophy and their curriculum is in terms of the actual inculcation of virtue. This is not a new point. Other scholars have emphasized the teaching of virtue in ancient Stoic schools.[31] One way in which students might have understood the relationship between Aedesius and Sosipatra, for instance, is that he taught the lower virtues and she the higher ones. But again, we cannot speculate too much about their respective curriculum given how little information Eunapius gives us.

The enumeration, definition, and ordering of virtues began with Plato, who argued for four virtues in the *Republic*, namely, temperance, courage, justice, and wisdom.[32] Plotinus agreed with Plato but added that these four virtues existed at two distinct levels: the "Political Virtues" (*politikai aretai*) existed "at the level of embodied life," and a "higher sort of these virtues, the Purificatory" (*kathartikai*), existed on the level of the intellect.[33] Plotinus found these virtues represented in the *Phaedo*

28. Dillon and Hershbell, *Iamblichus*, 22.

29. Eunap., *VS* 6.90–91.

30. Edward Jay Watts, *City and School in Late Antique Athens and Alexandria* (Berkeley: University of California Press, 2006), 4.

31. Pierre Hadot, *The Inner Citadel: The Meditations of Marcus Aurelius* (Cambridge, MA: Harvard University Press, 1998); Pierre Hadot, *Philosophy as a Way of Life: Spiritual Exercises from Socrates to Foucault* (Malden, MA: Blackwell, 1995).

32. John F. Finamore, "Iamblichus on the Grades of Virtue," in *Iamblichus and the Foundations of Late Platonism*, ed. E.V. Afonasin, John M. Dillon, and John F. Finamore (Leiden: Brill, 2012), 113.

33. Finamore, "Iamblichus on the Grades of Virtue," 113.

and argued that they led the soul "to the Intellect, where the paradigms of these four virtues pre-exist (*Enneads* 1.2)."[34]

In his *Sententiae* 32, Porphyry agreed with Plotinus regarding these two classes of virtue, the Political and the Purificatory, but he added two additional layers. Porphyry does not name the first of these but characterizes it as "higher than purification, when the soul after being purified attaches itself to the Intellect (32.33–62)."[35] The second he called "Paradigmatic" Virtues (*paradeigmatikai*). These "exist in the Intellect and serve as the paradigms for the soul's virtues (32.63–70)."[36] Not to be outdone by his predecessors, Iamblichus added yet three more levels to this hierarchy of virtues. He added the Natural (*physikai*), the Ethical (*ethikai*), and the Hieratic or Theurgic Virtues (*hieratikai/theurgikai*).[37] Iamblichus appears to have given the name "Contemplative Virtue" to Porphyry's unnamed virtue, and he ordered all seven levels of virtue from lowest to highest as follows: Natural, Ethical, Political, Purificatory, Contemplative, Paradigmatic, and Hieratic/Theurgic. As Damascius was aware of this Iamblichean schema in the fifth century CE, we can imagine that it was a persistent part of Platonic curriculum in this lineage and may well have been part of what Sosipatra taught to her students.

In addition to this exegetical activity based on a canon of classical philosophical texts, we might ask what else formed the curriculum of late ancient philosophy schools in the Neo-Pythagorean/Neo-Platonist lineages associated with Iamblichus and his followers. As we know from earlier chapters, the Iamblichan philosophical lineage incorporated ritual practices and what we might call sacred understandings of the goal of philosophy and human intellectual activity more generally, such as assimilation to the gods or divinization. This approach was known among contemporaries as theurgy, or god-work. We have already discussed some aspects of this approach and its relationship to the *Chaldean Oracles*, which were likely also part of Iamblichus's curriculum for more advanced students seeing as he wrote a long commentary on them.[38] But how did Eunapius think of the relationship between philosophy and theurgy in the context of the pedagogical enterprise? First, by the time of Porphyry and Iamblichus, and certainly until the time of

---

34. Finamore, "Iamblichus on the Grades of Virtue," 113.

35. Finamore, "Iamblichus on the Grades of Virtue," 113.

36. Finamore, "Iamblichus on the Grades of Virtue," 113.

37. Finamore, "Iamblichus on the Grades of Virtue," 113–14.

38. Dillon and Hershbell, *Iamblichus*, 22.

Proclus in the fifth century, theurgically inclined philosophers would have insisted that "Plato's divinely inspired . . . theology" was "in accord with the mystic traditions of Orpheus, Musaeus, Homer, and Hesiod, as well as the Assyrian [i.e., Chaldean] and ancient Egyptians sages."[39] It was also combined with Neo-Pythagorean thought. Iamblichus himself states that the "divine philosophy of Pythagoras being inseparable from cultic practices, is rather composite in its historical development: some things being learned from the Orphics, some from the Egyptian priests, some from the Chaldean mages, some from the Eleusinian rites . . ." (*Vita Pyth.* 84.14–18).[40] In other words, these later Platonists understood this synthesis to have occurred prior to Plato himself, whether or not that was actually the case.

Hence, by the time of Iamblichus and the philosophers in his lineage featured in Eunapius's biographies, theurgy or theurgically inclined and informed philosophy was understood to be the distillation of a number of philosophical and ritual/religious traditions. Of course, someone such as Iamblichus was making the claim to have a superior understanding of these traditions and practices in comparison with the everyday priests and ritual experts operating within these traditions who worked without the insight that came from sufficient education and care of the soul.[41] We might ask what this distillation looked like in practice. According to Iamblichus, the goal of theurgy was to purify and liberate the soul "from the bonds of generation, making us like to the gods and rendering us worthy to enjoy their friendship."[42] By bonds of generation, Iamblichus means both embodiment and cycles of reincarnation. For Iamblichus and his followers, theurgy included "all traditional liturgies, rites, and sacrifices which are ordained, revealed and in fact performed by the gods themselves."[43] By this Iamblichus means that the gods have both instituted ritual practices and embedded connections within and between levels of the cosmos that can be activated by these rituals. This activation enjoins the gods to respond:

39. Algis Uždavinys, *Philosophy and Theurgy in Late Antiquity* (Kettering: Angelico Press, 2010), 9.

40. Uždavinys, *Philosophy and Theurgy,* 19.

41. Heidi Marx-Wolf, *Spiritual Taxonomies and Ritual Authority: Platonists, Priests, and Gnostics in the Third Century C.E.* (Philadelphia: University of Pennsylvania Press, 2016), 100–125.

42. Iamb., *Myst.* 230.2.

43. Uždavinys, *Philosophy and Theurgy,* 82.

The awakened divine symbols by themselves perform their
holy work, thereby elevating the initiate to the gods whose
ineffable power (*dunamis*) recognizes by itself its own images
(*eikones*).[44]

Another way to understand this "system" is that "sacrifice and ritual make the soul suitable to receive divine providence which extends everywhere."[45] This theurgical understanding of assimilation to the gods is based on a cosmology and metaphysics that derived from ancient philosophical works such as the *Timaeus* and *Enneads*, and which emphasized the macro-microcosmic connections built into the fabric of the cosmos by the demiurge. These connections intersect at the level of all ensouled beings, but most importantly at the level of the human being, sitting as it does at the very ontological boundary between mortal and immortal, or animal and divine, even in some sense sublunary and supralunary, that is, the realms below and above the moon. In ancient cosmologies, the moon served as a kind of boundary between the realm of the highest gods and the realm of lower species of beings. Above the moon, the elements of fire and aether predominated, whereas below the moon, the grosser elements of earth, water, and air were present in greater proportions. In the supralunary realm, bodies had more perfect, circular shapes and moved in perfect circular patterns or orbits.

Educated philosophers had a special understanding of the connections between the human being and the greater cosmos, which they could use in their individual efforts to assimilate to the divine through ritual and which they could also leverage on behalf of the souls of others. In addition to the rituals associated with various traditional cults about which theurgists claimed to have special knowledge, they also engaged in more ad hoc, small-scale ritual activity themselves, a point we will discuss in more detail in Chapter 5. Furthermore, their participation in various initiation rituals was interpreted by Eunapius as a form of *paideia* (i.e., education). This was the case for the Emperor Julian's initiation into the mysteries of Eleusis as well as the initiation of Sosipatra's son, Antoninus, into the secret rites in honor of various gods at Canopis.[46] In sum, for Eunapius and his biographical subjects,

---

44. Uždavinys, *Philosophy and Theurgy*, 82.

45. Ilinca Tanaseanu-Döbler, *Theurgy in Late Antiquity: The Invention of a Ritual Tradition* (Göttingen: Vandenhoeck & Ruprecht, 2013), 149.

46. Tanaseanu-Döbler, *Theurgy in Late Antiquity*, 154.

"theurgy implies supernormal abilities and is intimately connected with the higher parts of philosophy, probably with theology and its practical consequences."[47]

What Did Sosipatra Teach?

As mentioned earlier, Eunapius discusses Sosipatra's teachings only once in passing. He says that she was lecturing on the nature of the soul, its descent, what part of it was subject to punishment, and what part of it was immortal.[48] At first glance, this doesn't seem like much information to work with. Yet these questions were at the core of a great deal of late Platonist philosophizing. They arose in the context of exegetical work on Platonic and Aristotelian texts. But they also emerged as topics for discussion when philosophers such as Porphyry and Iamblichus turned their attention to grappling hermeneutically with myth, oracle, and ritual.

When thinking about late Platonic thought on the nature of the soul, we are really dealing with a complex of interrelated questions: What is the soul's primordial state? Is it embodied, incorporeal, immaterial? How does it come to be embodied? For how long and if provisionally, what is the process by which it can disentangle itself from corporeality? These questions can be raised about human souls, in particular, but Platonic speculation extended to a whole range of souls, including those of animals, good and evil daemons, heroes, angels, archons, demigods, gods, and the souls of the celestial bodies such as planets and stars. In fact, there was a great deal of movement between these levels in the Platonic cosmos, souls descending from and ascending to the celestial realms both in terms of their primordial entrance into the sublunary sphere according to Platonic myth and also in terms of cycles of reincarnation. Sosipatra could have been talking about either of these situations—the soul's initial entry into a body or its reentry in the context of reincarnation. Given she is also discussing the soul's punishment, it is likely the latter. But it will be helpful to give an overview of the main questions and concepts in Platonic thinking related to both situations.

47. Tanaseanu-Döbler, *Theurgy in Late Antiquity*, 154.
48. Eunap., *VS* 6.91.

It is possible to trace the impetus for philosophical speculation about questions of embodiment back to Plato himself who posed the problem in a variety of ways in his dialogues and offered multiple, sometimes conflicting, explanations for why and how different kinds of souls inhabit bodies of various sorts, but in particular human ones. Platonists had to struggle to make sense of an apparent contradiction between two main accounts of embodiment in the works of Plato. The *Timaeus* argued that the soul "had a constructive mission in the world to vivify, organize, and perfect it."[49] We see this in the "likely story" told in the *Timaeus* not only at the level of the World Soul or Demiurge, but also at the level of the gods the Demiurge creates to order the levels of creation below them. We see this kind of thinking reflected in Porphyry's description of good daemons in *On Abstinence from Animals* where he writes the following:

> All the souls which, having issued from the universal soul,
> administer large parts of the regions below the moon, resting
> on their *pneuma* but controlling it by reason, should be
> regarded as good *daimones* who do everything for the benefit
> of those they rule, whether they are in charge of certain
> animals, or of crops which have been assigned to them, or of
> what happens for the sake of these—showers of rain, moderate
> winds, fine weather, and the balance of the seasons within the
> year; or again, for our sake, they are in charge of skills, or of
> all kinds of education in the liberal arts, or of medicine and
> physical training and other such things.[50]

It is this Timaean notion of ensoulment/embodiment that informed Plotinus's emanational schema as well, that is, his model whereby lower orders of the cosmos emerge from higher ones, emanating from them all the way from the highest One down to the lowest level of the cosmos.

On the other hand, the *Phaedrus* tells a competing myth, the myth of the winged soul, which "due to some moral failure" falls "from the heavenly retinue of the gods" and is "plunged into a life of misery in the body."[51] This fall is echoed in Porphyry's description of evil daemons in

---

49. Dominic O'Meara, *Pythagoras Revived: Mathematics and Philosophy in Late Antiquity* (Oxford: Oxford University Press, 1991), 38.

50. Porph., *Abst.* 2.38.2. Porphyry, *On Abstinence from Killing Animals*, trans. Gillian Clark (Ithaca, NY: Cornell University Press, 2000), 71.

51. O'Meara, *Pythagoras Revived*, 38.

On Abstinence. Evil daemons are good daemons who have succumbed to the appetites and passions associated with their "bodies," which he refers to as pneumatic vessels or chariots. On account of indulgence, these become heavier and denser due to accretions of moist, damp air from the sublunary realm, causing the soul to sink into lower levels of this realm.[52]

Origen of Alexandria, a Christian Platonist who some scholars think was a fellow student of Ammonius Saccas with Plotinus, described something similar regarding all souls in his *On First Principles*. He argued that embodiment of various kinds, whether human, angelic, or demonic, was the response of the Divine or One to the loss of ardor for God experienced to varying degrees by all primordial Minds or Intelligences, all of whom had been created equal. This is how Origen interpreted Hebrew Scripture's myths of the creation and fall, drawing on Platonic ideas for exegetical principles. This sort of hermeneutic activity in relation to myth is taken up by non-Christian Platonists as well. For instance, Porphyry applied his exegetical skill to the Homeric accounts of the Cave of the Nymphs and the River Styx in various treatises. In each case, his interpretive efforts were focused on the problem of embodiment, and in his treatment of the Styx, he also focused on the questions of punishment, reward, and reincarnation. In other words, Platonist thinking not only had to deal with the question of why souls were embodied in a primordial sense. It also had to deal with the question of why souls were embodied repeatedly and as different sorts of creatures.

Once again, Plato's own myths served as the basis for some of this speculation on reincarnation. At the end of the *Republic* (10.614–10.621), Socrates tells the story of Er, son of Armenius, who after being killed in battle remained unburied for ten days. His body was undecayed, and he came to life again upon his funeral pyre. He told the people gathered about what he had seen in the other world. What follows in the *Republic* is a complex myth about where souls go after their life on earth (either to places of bliss and reward or to places of punishment and correction based on how they lived) and how they reenter this world through a process of reincarnation (based in part on Necessity and, in part, on their own choices for the kind of life they would like to lead next). The richness and complexity of this myth allowed for almost endless exegesis

---

52. Porph., *Abst.* 2.42.3.

and philosophical speculation about why souls come to be embodied as they are and where they go after this life.

Not surprisingly, later Platonists in the lineage Eunapius records felt the need to grapple with the Myth of Er exegetically. One of the more interesting examples of this is a pair of fragmentary texts from Porphyry of Tyre entitled *On What is in Our Power* and *To Gaurus on How Embryos Are Ensouled.* The title of the first work refers to the problem posed by the Myth of Er, namely, how much power a soul has to choose its next life in the cycle of reincarnation both in terms of the kind of ontological status it will have (animal, human, etc.) and what the circumstances of that life will be. Another way to ask the question is in terms of the degree to which reincarnating souls are conditioned or constrained by the kind of life they led in their former existence on earth in combination with the time they spent after this life either in the sky (a place of bliss and reward) or underground (a place of punishment). These experiences left the soul marked or stained in ways that certainly limited choice, according to both the Myth of Er and Porphyry's interpretation of it. But choice was also limited, according to Porphyry, at the cosmic level in accordance with the way the physical workings of the heavenly movements opened up different portals for souls to enter based on ancient astrological understandings.[53] In Porphyry's thinking, we see an intersection between Platonic myth interpreted rather literally and late ancient Chaldean understandings of astrology. In *On What s in Our Power*, Porphyry viewed this process, namely, the process of ensoulment in the context of reincarnation, from the side of the soul descending into a new life. In his work, *To Gaurus on How Emrbyos Are Ensouled,* he seems to have considered the same moment from the side of the body that receives an incarnating soul. In this work, Porphyry argued that the embryo was, in essence, a plant until the moment of its birth, when it called down a soul appropriate to it from the upper regions of the sublunary realm where souls await descent.[54] Here too we see similar astrological ideas at work, because the cosmos plays the role of matchmaker between souls and bodies fit for them based on portals

53. James Wilberding, *Porphyry: To Gaurus on How Embryos Are Ensouled and On What Is in Our Power* (Bristol: Bristol Classical Press, 2011), 119–70.

54. Wilberding, *Porphyry,* 1–117; Heidi Marx-Wolf, "Medicine," in *Late Ancient Knowing,* ed. Catherine Chin and Moulie Vidas (Berkeley: University of California Press, forthcoming); Heidi Marx-Wolf, "Living Plants, Dead Animals, and Other Matters: Embryos and Demons in Porphyry of Tyre," *Preternature: Critical and Historical Studies on the Preternatural* 7, no. 1 (March 16, 2018): 1–26.

opening in the heavens as the celestial bodies move through various astrological positions. To put it crudely, the movement of the heavenly spheres acts like a kind of soul dispensary. Similar ideas are found in the works of Iamblichus, as noted when we discussed the daemonic or angelic nature of Sosipatra's Chaldean teachers.[55]

We cannot know which of these many ideas may have informed Sosipatra's teaching on these very complex philosophical questions. But this brief overview of the many ideas in circulation at the time at least provides us with a taste of the richness and variation available to her within her particular lineage. Eunapius's estimation of her superiority as a teacher indicates that he wished his readers to think of her as a leading light in the Iamblichean lineage when it came to teaching on standard Platonic topics. Her engagement with Chaldean thought as a young girl should also point us in the direction of writers such as Porphyry and Iamblichus who actively sought to harmonize Platonic ideas with Chaldean teachings, if we wish to understand how she may have approached the topics Eunapius tells us were themes in her classroom. In Chapter 5, we will consider how she may have put some of these ideas into practice when it came to her ritual and prophetic activity.

---

55. Sarah Iles Johnston, "Working Overtime in the Afterlife; or, No Rest for the Virtuous," in *Heavenly Realms and Earthly Realities in Late Antique Religions*, ed. Annette Yoshiko Reed and Ra'anan S. Boustan (Cambridge: Cambridge University Press, 2004), 85–100.

5

Sosipatra as a Theurgist and Oracle

We have already noted a number of times that philosophy, and in particular Neo-Platonic thought in the lineage of Iamblichus (which Eunapius traced back through Porphyry to Plotinus, Ammonius Saccas, and ultimately Plato), took on a religious and theological focus and emphasized engagement with ritual practices that would aid lovers of wisdom in their pursuit of truth in the form of assimilation to and unity with the highest gods. It is clear from Eunapius's discussion of Sosipatra's education and initiation into Chaldaean *paideia*, and her teaching as a philosopher in Pergamum, that he saw her as an exemplary figure in the Iamblichean lineage of ritually engaged Platonism—that is, theurgy. It is the aim of this chapter to consider Sosipatra's place in the larger school of theurgically inclined philosophical practitioners and to consider what she might represent in Eunapius's narrative, what meaning she has for him not just as a teacher of philosophy but as a divine or holy figure compared with other similar figures in the *Lives*, both male and female. It is important to keep in mind, though, that her teaching and spiritual activities would not have been understood as distinct in the way that we tend to think about the difference between philosophical teaching and spirituality today. Today it is common to juxtapose the rationality of philosophical forms of thinking with the irrationality of religious belief or spiritual activity. For philosophers in the Iamblichean lineage, however, rationality and revelation (especially in the form of divination) were understood to be complimentary and interpenetrating. Theurgy, as we are referring to it, was not irrational, but rather it was the "culmination and transcendence of rationality."[1] Another way we can think

1. Crystal Addey, *Divination and Theurgy in Neoplatonism: Oracles of the Gods*, Ashgate Studies in Philosophy and Theology in Late Antiquity (Burlington, VT: Routledge, 2014), 31.

about this is that rationality represented the pinnacle of human thinking about the cosmos, and revelation, along with assimilation to divinity or divinization, allowed individuals to understand universal truths from a higher perspective, namely, a divine one.

To understand the nature of Sosipatra's identity as a divine woman and the relationship of her status to various kinds of religious activity or ritual in addition to philosophical expertise and aptitude, we need to discuss the variety of ritual expertise represented among holy men and women in antiquity in general and among various figures in Eunapius's narrative in particular. This will allow us to understand what the relationship between theurgy and philosophy is for Eunapius and to draw comparisons between figures within the text. We will see that in many important respects, Eunapius holds Sosipatra up as the ideal or perfect exemplar of theurgical expertise. And, as mentioned in the introduction, he uses her, on the one hand, to critique the excesses of others (both other theurgists and Christian ascetics), and on the other, to caution readers about the times in which they live, times which Eunapius perceived as hostile to theurgically inclined, non-Christian philosophy and to the polytheistic worship its practitioners considered critical to maintaining the proper and harmonious order between cosmic levels, and in particular between humans and gods.

*Ritual Activity and Miracles in the Lives of Divine Men
and Women*

As already noted, ritual activities and practices, divination being the most important of these, were not considered irrational or at odds with philosophical forms of reasoning. Rather, they were understood in the Iamblichean milieu to be by their very nature complementary to reason and the culmination and transcendence of rationality.[2] Participation in ritual activities was not understood to be a devolution into irrational superstition or the perversion of a purely rational approach to philosophical wisdom.[3] Rather, divination and other

2. Addey, *Divination and Theurgy*, 31.
3. This was the view of an earlier generation of scholars, such as E. R. Dodds. But this view has been significantly challenged by scholars such as Gregory Shaw, Polymnia Athanassiadi, and myself.

miraculous experiences in the lives of late ancient philosophers and sages were understood to be evidence of their assimilation to divinity and recognition by the gods and other spirits of their holiness. This is the reason that most if not all intellectual biographies of this period focus on miraculous moments and experiences in the lives of their subjects. But it is not enough to just take note of the presence of these accounts in the works of authors such as Eunapius, because these episodes are usually crafted in particular ways to make arguments about the respective holiness of the figures discussed. In other words, not all records of miraculous moments in the hagiographical accounts of holy men and women are doing the same kind of work in the text.[4] And some of these stories are instrumental in establishing hierarchies of "saints" within and between texts.[5] Readers must pay careful attention to the rhetoric of storytelling, to parodic elements, to exaggeration, to subtle criticism, and so forth in order to get a sense of how authors are positioning their subjects in relation to each other within texts or to others in the biographical works of competing authors. In the case of philosophers, who are also holy men and women, the place to look for this argument about positionality is often in accounts of their miraculous activities and experiences.

To understand the miraculous aspects of Sosipatra's biography and the arguments Eunapius endeavors to make by relating them, we need to place them also within the genre of ancient philosophical biography. To limit this frame somewhat, I will begin with works produced by or about the philosophers Eunapius includes in his lineage, namely, Plotinus, Porphyry, and Iamblichus. But it is helpful to note that Philostratus's lively portrait of Apollonius of Tyana, the Pythagorean philosopher, wonderworker, and holy man, serves as an important precursor and model for the kind of biographical writing Eunapius engages in. Front and center in Philostratus's work are his subject's association with temples, worships, and other holy men and women as well as his miraculous displays of his own divine identity and assimilation to divinity.

---

4. The most important monograph on late ancient biography in this regard is Patricia Cox Miller, *Biography in Late Antiquity: A Quest for the Holy Man*, Transformation of the Classical Heritage, 5 (Berkeley: University of California Press, 1983).

5. See, for instance, Virginia Burrus, *The Sex Lives of the Saints: An Erotics of Ancient Hagiography* (Philadelphia: University of Pennsylvania Press, 2004), 24–33.

For our purposes, we can start with a few episodes in the life of Plotinus written by his student Porphyry, episodes that highlight Plotinus's divine identity and nature. Porphyry's biography of Plotinus is important for our reading of Eunapius's telling of Sosipatra's life because there are moments, especially those related to divine revelation, ritual participation, and miraculous events in her life that seem to be patterned on or in dialogue with moments in the life of Plotinus. For instance, Porphyry records a number of instances in which events conspired to reveal Plotinus's divine status. On one occasion, for instance, Plotinus agreed to accompany an Egyptian priest who had come to Rome to the temple of Isis where "the latter intended to reveal a visible manifestation of the philosopher's indwelling *daimon*."[6] In this moment, we witness Plotinus's participation in a ritual of invocation. According to Porphyry, Plotinus's indwelling spirit turned out to be a god and "not a companion of the subordinate order," a distinction that will be reinforced in Sosipatra's divination of her husband's indwelling spirit and her own.[7] Exactly which god Plotinus's spirit was associated with remained a mystery, "as the friend who was taking part in the manifestation strangled the birds which he was holding as a protection, either out of jealousy or because he was afraid of something."[8] In a similar fashion, just when Sosipatra comes close to revealing the nature of her daemon or divine spirit, she is prevented by a revelation, an injunction from this very indwelling spirit.[9] This episode warrants further discussion later in this chapter, but for now it is important to note the similarities between Porphyry's *Life of Plotinus* and Eunapius's account of Sosipatra, both of which also evoke episodes in the life of Socrates when his inner daemon delivered injunctions and revelations.

Another episode in Plotinus's life may have also served as a prototype for Eunapius. In this episode, Plotinus is depicted as deflecting the spell of a rival named Olympius of Alexandria, another student of Plotinus's teacher, Ammonius Saccas. Porphyry writes, "This man's attacks on him

---

6. Heidi Wendt, *At the Temple Gates: The Religion of Freelance Experts in the Roman Empire* (Oxford: Oxford University Press, 2016), 83.

7. Porph., *Plot.* 10. (Plotinus, *Porphyry on Plotinus. Ennead I*, trans. A. H. Armstrong [Cambridge, MA: Harvard University Press, 1966], 35.)

8. Porph., *Plot.* 10.

9. Eunap., *VS* 6.78.

went to the point of trying to bring a star-stroke upon him by magic."[10] Olympius, however, found his efforts "recoiling upon himself" because of Plotinus's great powers that were "able to throw back attacks on him on to those who were seeking to do him harm."[11] This episode is mirrored in the biography of Sosipatra, when her kinsmen, Philometer, casts a binding spell on her, causing her to fall in love with him.[12] The differences in the way Plotinus and Sosipatra handle their respective attacks is interesting. Plotinus's greatness makes him impervious to the attack, but Sosipatra suffers and employs her student Maximus to undertake rituals that will release her from the spell.[13] We will discuss this episode more later in this chapter as well. In the case of Plotinus, what is interesting is that we see a rival philosopher engaged in casting harmful spells ostensibly to give himself a competitive professional advantage. And we see Plotinus rebuff the attempt not through rational discourse but through an exhibition of his spiritual power and divine status.

We also witness the importance of oracles, that is, divine revelation and communication, in the *Life of Plotinus* after he dies. Amelius, another of Plotinus's most devoted students, consulted Apollo and asked where the soul of Plotinus had gone. Porphyry relates the oracle in its entirety after reminding his readers of what Apollo had said of Socrates, namely, that he was the wisest of men. Apollo had, in the intervening centuries, become far more loquacious, so it seems. After recounting the greatness of Plotinus's life and emphasizing the way in which it was guided and informed by direct divine intervention, the oracle rewards Amelius with a detailed explanation of the final resting place of his teacher's soul:

> But now that you have been freed from this tabernacle and
> have left the tomb which held your heavenly soul, you come at
> once to the company of heaven, where winds of delight blow,
> where is affection and desire that charms the sight, full of pure
> joy, brimming with streams of immortality from the gods
> which carry the allurements of the Loves, and sweet breeze
> and the windless brightness of high heaven. There dwell Minos
> and Rhadamanthus, brethren of the Golden race of great Zeus,

---

10. Porph., *Plot.* 10. The verb is *astroboleiomai* (trans. Armstrong, 35).
11. Porph., *Plot.* 10 (trans. Armstrong, 35).
12. Eunap., *VS* 6.82.
13. Eunap., *VS* 6.83–85.

there righteous Aeacus and Plato, the sacred power, and noble
Pythagoras and all who have set the dance of the immortal
love and won kinship with spirits most blessed, there where
the heart keeps festival in everlasting joy. O blessed one, you
have borne so many contests, and now move among holy
spirits, crowned with the mighty life.[14]

This view of the celestial home of the philosopher's soul would have
informed Eunapius's understanding of Sosipatra's post-mortem fate as
well, especially given the fact that she foretells that her husband's soul
will rise to the lunar realm, but hers will rise higher. It is likely that
Eunapius thought her soul would keep the same company as Plotinus's
after her death.

Late Ancient Biographies of Pythagoras

In addition to writing his *Life of Plotinus*, Porphyry wrote other
biographies of important philosophers, including the pre-Socratic
sage, Pythagoras. By the time he was producing these works, many
philosophers thought of Pythagoras as an important precursor to and
influence on Plato, and hence as part of the same lineage. Iamblichus
thought of Pythagoras in this way as well and also wrote a biographical
work on him. In Porphyry's case, his vita was but one sketch in a longer
work containing the lives of other philosophers. But Iamblichus wrote
an entire work, entitled *On the Pythagorean Way of Life*. In this work,
he not only recorded stories about Pythagoras's life and teachings, but
he also discussed events related to the philosopher's followers and their
style of living as part of Pythagoras's school and community. This work
was a preface to a series of other pedagogically oriented works that set
out a kind of Pythagorean curriculum, probably for Iamblichus's own
students. It is very likely that Iamblichus wrote this set of Pythagorean
works to compete with Porphyry, who had written the *Life of Plotinus*
and edited and compiled the *Enneads*.[15] In other words, each wrote a

---

14. Porph., *Plot.* 22 (trans. Armstrong, 67–69).

15. Heidi Marx-Wolf, "Pythagoras the Theurgist: Porphyry and Iamblichus on the Role of
Ritual in the Philosophical Life," in *Religious Competition in the Third Century* CE: *Jews, Christians,
and the Greco-Roman World*, ed. Jordan Rosenblum, Lily Vuong, and Nathaniel DesRosiers
(Göttingen: Vandenhoeck & Ruprecht, 2014), 32–33.

biography of an important philosophical figure as an introduction to a set of pedagogical works or school texts. These biographies then function as foundational documents to lend authority to the teaching activities of their authors.

Iamblichus's *On the Pythagorean Way of Life* is of particular interest to us in its idealized and imaginative portrait of a philosophical holy man. It also presents an idealized picture of a philosophical community with a clear ritual focus. Iamblichus likely highlights ritual in the life and school of Pythagoras as much as he does to give more weight to his own theurgical focus. He supplies his reader with all kinds of details about the many prescriptions Pythagoras shared with his students related to living a philosophical life, a good life, and which he enjoined them to adopt themselves. These included guidance about dress, worship, diet, sleep, and other habits. For instance, according to Iamblichus, the students of Pythagoras were to meet in temples for their instruction, and they were to follow a strict regimen involving light exercise, simple food for lunch, an afternoon walk, a daily bath, and a simple evening meal before which they made offerings of libations, aromatic herbs, and incense.[16] After dinner, Pythagoras would put his students to bed by playing music for them, thereby banishing the disharmony of the day. He would also wake them up in the morning in this way. Iamblichus may have thought about this music as hymns for the gods. He also portrayed Pythagoras teaching about proper ritual on numerous occasions. For instance, when teaching the citizens of Croton, he taught the women of the city how to properly prepare their offerings to the gods with their own hands, namely, "round cakes, cakes of ground barley, honey combs and incense," and to offer them without slaves.[17]

Iamblichus also recorded or possibly invented a legend about the priest of Apollo, Abaris, who upon meeting Pythagoras, "recognized in him a particular likeness to the god whose priest he was."[18] Abaris, being convinced that Pythagoras was Apollo, and "not just a mortal resembling that god," gave him an arrow with a number of miraculous properties:

16. Iambl., *VPyth.* 21.

17. Iambl., *VPyth.* 11.54 (trans. John Dillon and Jackson P. Hershbell, *Iamblichus: On the Pythagorean Way of Life*, Society of Biblical Literature, Texts and Translations 29 [Atlanta: Scholars Press, 1991], 79).

18. Iambl., *VPyth.* 19.91 (trans. Dillon and Hershbell, 115).

For riding on it he crossed impassible places; for example, rivers, lakes, swamps, mountains, and the like. And talking to the arrow, so goes the story, he performed purifications and drove off plagues and winds from the cities which asked for his assistance.[19]

Iamblichus's portrait of Pythagoras and his philosophical "school" is one that may never have been realized in Pythagoras's time, nor in Iamblichus's or Sosipatra's for that matter. But his total care for his students and followers through various ritual means, means that activated the sympathetic and harmonic connections built into the cosmos for the benefit of human souls, would have served as a kind of ideal for leaders of some late ancient philosophy schools.

Theurgical, Ritual, and Miraculous Activity in Eunapius's Lives

When we turn directly to Eunapius, we observe his consistent habit of relaying any information he has, much of it likely based in oral tradition, about events that provide evidence of the divine and holy character of his subjects and their assimilation to the gods.[20] Porphyry does not receive a lot of attention in this regard, but his own works speak to his avid interest in divination and oracles. He collected oracles and interpreted them philosophically (see, for instance, his *Philosophy from Oracles*). He did the same with Homeric myths (see, for instance, *On the Cave of the Nymphs* and *On the River Styx*) and with Platonic myths (see, for instance, his interpretations of the Myth of Er found in his works *To Gaurus on the Ensoulment of Embryos* and *On What Is in Our Power*). So he was himself interested in communication and communion between human souls and higher spirits, and in the processes by which the former are assimilated to the latter. In Eunapius's account of Porphyry's life, he only tells us that Porphyry once performed an exorcism of a daemon that was called Kausatha by the inhabitants of the town. This daemon had taken residence in a local bathing establishment.[21] Porphyry, according to Eunapius, also claimed to have been granted an

19. Iambl., *VPyth.* 19.91 (trans. Dillon and Hershbell, 115).
20. Edward Jay Watts, "Orality and Communal Identity in Eunapius' Lives of the Sophists and Philosophers," *Byzantion*, no. 75 (2005): 334–61.
21. Eunap., *VS* 4.12.

oracle "different from the vulgar sort," that is, one with philosophical or theological significance, and supposedly wrote about it expounding "at considerable length how men ought to pay attention to these oracles."[22]

Eunapius has more to say about the miraculous aspects of Iamblichus's biography. For instance, he relates that Iamblichus's slaves spread the rumor that their master levitated ten cubits above the ground when praying and that his garments glowed with a golden hue at the same time. When Iamblichus's students confronted him with this rumor, their teacher laughed and told them that from now on they could be present when he prayed.[23] Although Iamblichus denied that this happened to him when he prayed, both his slaves and his students expected that someone as holy as Iamblichus could levitate. Plotinus, according to Porphyry, claimed to have departed his body on a number of occasions to commune with higher spirits, and there are examples of sages levitating in Philostratus's *Life of Apollonius*. This is all to say that this rumor was in keeping with what people at the time expected of holy men and women.

While Eunapius left it ambiguous as to whether Iamblichus levitated while praying, he did record other miraculous events witnessed by students. The first of these Eunapius introduced as a true manifestation of Iamblichus's divine nature. Upon returning to the city from performing certain rites that had been prepared at one of Iamblichus's suburban villas (recall that Iamblichus was from a very wealthy family according to Eunapius), he broke from conversing about the gods and stopped. After some time during which he gazed at the ground lost in a kind of altered state, he said to his companions, "Let us go by another road for a dead body has lately been carried along this way."[24] Some of his more curious students, sensing Iamblichus's pronouncement was the result of some form of revelation and "scenting like hounds for the proof" decided to wait and find out more.[25] Eventually the company who had buried the dead man returned and the students questioned them to confirm the transport of the corpse earlier. What is interesting about this episode is not just that it is meant to highlight Iamblichus's cosmic attunement to disharmonious and polluting events, but it also

22. Eunap., *VS* 4.11 (trans. Wilmer Cave Wright, *Philostratus and Eunapius: The Lives of the Sophists* [Cambridge, MA: Harvard University Press, 1989], 359).

23. Eunap., *VS* 5.8–11.

24. Eunap., *VS* 5.12–14 (trans. Wright, 367).

25. Eunap., *VS* 5.15 (trans. Wright, 369).

signals a kind of fastidiousness about purity and the desire to reduce exposure to potentially corrupting influences.

In another episode, Iamblichus and his students were visiting some hot spring baths at a place called Gadara when they pestered him (as was their habit) to perform some sort of miracle, or give some evidence of his divine nature. In response to their cajoling, he smiled and said, "It is irreverent to the gods to give you this demonstration, but for your sakes it will be done."[26] He told his disciples to ask the locals what the names of the two springs were called. The answer was Eros and Anteros. Using this knowledge of the names, Iamblichus invoked the spirits of the springs. He touched the water in each, one after the other, and uttered a summons. Two boys emerged, alike in all respects except for the color of their hair (Figure 5.1). They embraced Iamblichus and "clung closely to him as though he were a real father."[27] He then "restored them to their proper places" and took his bath.[28] Presumably, Iamblichus's invocation of the water spirits was not entirely irreverent given the way the local manifestations of Eros and Anteros recognized in Iamblichus a parental figure of sorts, signaling a recognition of his divinity. In other words, his invocation was not a form of coercive magic, but in keeping with the natural cosmic order and its sympathetic connections.

After recording these miracles, Eunapius writes: "Even more astonishing and marvelous things were related of him but I wrote down none of these since I thought it a hazardous and sacrilegious thing to introduce a spurious and fluid tradition into a stable and well-founded narrative."[29] This tells us that Eunapius was working with certain criteria to determine which legends and traditions he deemed credible and important.

There are a number of instances in Eunapius's *Lives* where we see philosophers consulting with oracles instead of waiting for divinity to reveal itself without ritual prompting. Ideally, at least in the Eunapian understanding of divine assimilation, higher spirits respond to the fitness and purity of the theurgist's soul spontaneously. But in the examples that follow, we see philosophers engaged in processes that are meant to elicit divine responses. For instance, Aedesius, Sosipatra's friend and estate manager, in an earlier period in his life, was trying to determine

26. Eunap., *VS* 5.16–17 (trans. Wright, 369).
27. Eunap., *VS* 5.18–21 (trans. Wright, 371).
28. Eunap., *VS* 5.22 (trans. Wright, 371).
29. Eunap., *VS* 5.22. (trans. Wright, 371).

FIGURE 5.1 Statuette of Eros and Anteros embracing, Hellenistic Period. Ephesus Museum. Courtesy of the author. Photo by author.

what kind of life to lead. He prayed for a divine message, which came to him in hexameter verse in a dream.[30] Upon awakening, he realized that his understanding of the divine message was slipping away from him. He called out for a slave in order to wash his hands and face quickly so that he could turn to remembering the oracle. The slave noticed that there was writing covering the back of Aedesius's left hand. It was the oracular message, the substance of which was that if Aedesius remained in the city, he would be famous among men, but if he were to depart for a quiet life in the countryside, he would "one day be the associate of the blessed immortals."[31] He chose the latter and found a small estate in Cappadocia where he became a goatherd. His pastoral life was cut short, however, by the pestering of would-be students who called for his return to the province of Asia Minor where he set up a school in Pergamum, as we know.[32]

Eunapius records another instance where two of his subjects, Maximus of Ephesus and Chrysanthius, both students of Aedesius, and possibly of Sosipatra as well, consulted with the gods together to determine whether they should heed a summons from the Emperor Julian to join him at court just after his defeat of Constantius. It is likely they would have done this at an oracular temple in the vicinity.

Their consultation yielded "forbidding and hostile omens," to which Chrysanthius responded by saying, "Not only must I stay here, beloved Maximus, I must also hide myself from all men."[33] Maximus, on the other hand, countered by saying:

> Nay, Chrysanthius, I think you have forgotten that we have
> been educated to believe that it is the duty of genuine Hellenes,
> especially if they are learned men, not to yield absolutely to
> the first obstacles they meet; but rather to wrestle with the
> heavenly powers till you make them incline to their servant.[34]

Eunapius then tells us that when Chrysanthius departed, Maximus "remained and tried every method till he obtained the results he wished and desired."[35] In other words, he coerced the gods or cosmic forces

---

30. Eunap., *VS* 6.32.
31. Eunap., *VS* 6.33–34 (trans. Wright, 393).
32. Eunap., *VS* 6.35–38.
33. Eunap., *VS* 7.36–38 (trans. Wright, 441).
34. Eunap., *VS* 7.39 (trans. Wright, 441).
35. Eunap., *VS* 7.40 (trans. Wright, 443).

to give their assent to his desired aims, namely, to join Julian at court. This likely implies that he engaged in some form of coercive ritual practices that would have been classified by other theurgically inclined philosophers as "magic." It is important to note that this is not the only episode Eunapius recounts of Maximus's hubristic tendencies.

Maximus is also the only person in Eunapius's text to engage in a ritual practice that would become far more prominent in later forms of theurgy, namely, statue animation or the telestic arts, that is, rituals to incite a god or goddess to inhabit his or her statue. Although this practice is discussed in other texts, Eunapius's description is one of the most detailed accounts we have of the practice.

The story is told by Eusebius, a fellow student with Maximus and Chrysanthius in the school of Aedesius. Eusebius also served as a teacher to the Emperor Julian along with Chrysanthius. The story he told inspired Julian to leave these teachers and seek out Maximus in Ephesus instead. According to Eusebius, Maximus invited him and others in the school to a temple of Hecate and thereby "produced many witnesses of his folly."[36] Hecate was a goddess of particular importance to theurgists.[37] In the temple, once everyone was seated, Maximus burned incense and recited a hymn. To the astonishment and terror of his audience, the statue of the goddess began to smile and the torches she held in her hands "burst into flame."[38]

Eusebius tried to remind everyone present at his telling of this story that these kinds of theatrical performances were less important than the "purification of the soul which is attained by reason."[39] But he failed to convince the future emperor, who kissed the head of his teacher Chrysanthius and left immediately for Ephesus in search of Maximus. Eunapius uses episodes that highlight Maximus's hubris, especially his efforts to coerce the gods instead of making himself receptive and fitting for their communication by the arduous work of purifying and transforming the soul, to explain why Maximus and Julian both suffered the fates they did and, I would argue, he uses them as foils for highlighting the extraordinary virtues of Sosipatra in particular.

36. Eunap., *VS* 7.22 (trans. Wright, 435).

37. Sarah Iles Johnston, *Hekate Soteira: A Study of Hekate's Role in the Chaldean Oracles and Related Literature*, American Classical Studies 21 (Atlanta: Scholars Press, 1990).

38. Eunap., *VS* 7.23 (trans. Wright, 435).

39. Eunap., *VS* 7.25 (trans. Wright, 435).

We have already discussed a number of episodes in Sosipatra's life that involve her in theurgical activities, that is, activities that either bring her closer in nature and connection to divinity or that reveal her already established divine status. Her education by Chaldeans is the first of these, a process that was more akin to an initiation into mysteries than a traditional schooling process. Ten years old when her father returned to his estate after his five-year absence, Sosipatra was capable of remotely viewing the journey he took to come back to her.

The second major episode Eunapius relates that speaks to Sosipatra's theurgical status is the prophecy she delivered on the occasion of her marriage to Eustathius. As we know, she prophesied that her husband would live a few more years, long enough to produce three sons. Then she informed those gathered that his soul would rise to the level of the lunar sphere, stating "for so does your phantom say to me," thereby referring to Eustathius's daemon.[40] Hers, she also told her listeners, would rise even higher. But she is prevented from disclosing the specific location by her "god," her "divine double," we might say.[41] This is a concept to which we will return in a moment. But first we should explore this prophetic moment in more detail to see how it fits with other oracular pronouncements in the lives of philosophers and other moments of celestial ascent while inhabiting a human body. In other words, it is helpful to explore the various late ancient frameworks that Eunapius's readers might have relied on to understand this particular episode. We have already considered the case of the oracle related by Amelius to Porphyry regarding Plotinus's post-mortem fate. But Sosipatra foretells and foresees where her and her husband's souls will go, presumably having had some sort of direct experience of it. We have numerous examples of what we might refer to as celestial journeys from ancient literature. One of the earliest of these is Cicero's *Dream of Scipio*. The apotheosis of emperors is another example of popular ideas about celestial ascent after death.

Porphyry also talked about Plotinus's soul leaving his body on four occasions during his life, presumably to travel to higher cosmic realms.

40. Eunap., *VS* 6.77.

41. This concept of the "divine double" is most thoroughly explored in Charles M. Stang, *Our Divine Double* (Cambridge, MA: Harvard University Press, 2016).

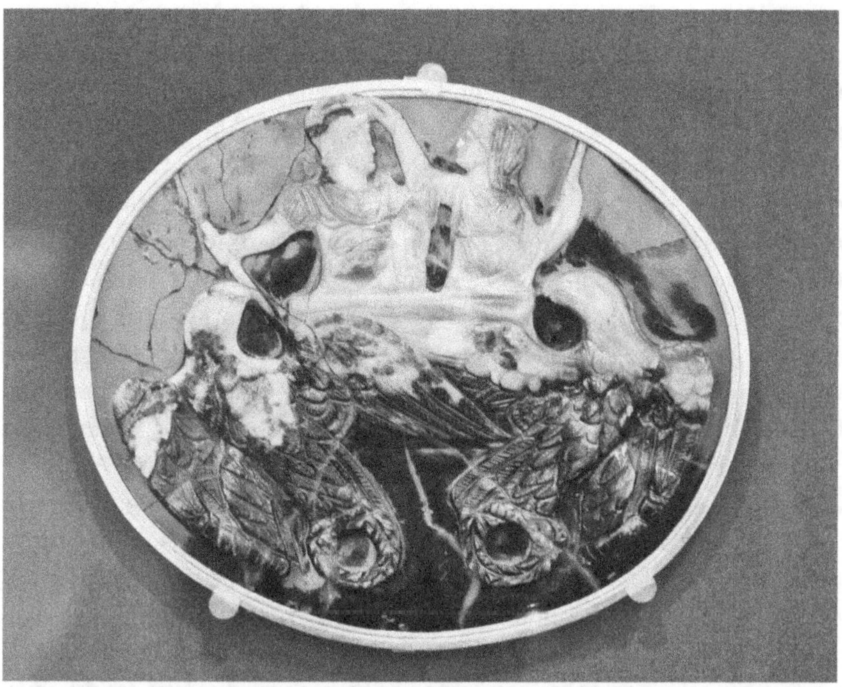

FIGURE 5.2 Cameo of the apotheosis of Trajan, second century CE, Staatliche Muzeen zu Berlin. Courtesy of the author. Photo by author.

And we have already discussed the oracle regarding his post-mortem celestial ascent. Additionally, a number of Nag Hammadi works, such as *Zostrianos*, relate visions of souls ascending through various celestial regions and encountering en route the spirits that inhabit those places. We might even think of the moment in Augustine's *Confessions* when he and his mother Monica are sitting in a window overlooking a garden and have a shared visionary experience of rising up above the realm of material objects along the chain of being to the upper regions of the cosmos and more purified, divine ontological realms as standing in this tradition.[42] This is all to say that Sosipatra's ability to experience in advance the celestial journey of her husband's soul and her own is in keeping with late ancient understandings of both post-mortem expectations for especially holy people and the prophetic activities of these people in this life.

42. Aug., *Conf.* 9.10.23–26. Gillian Clark, *Monica: An Ordinary Saint*, Women in Antiquity (New York: Oxford University Press, 2015), 113–15.

To turn to the matter of the "divine double" in ancient thought, we can recall that Sosipatra is prevented from sharing the entirety of her vision by a guiding spirit, her "god" as she calls it. This is one of the few references to what we might call the "divine double" in Eunapius's work. But it is a common theme in Platonic literature. We need only think of the role that Socrates's daemon plays in the Platonic dialogues relating to his teacher's trial and death. We can also call to mind Plotinus's visit to the Temple of Isis where the priest was about to reveal the philosopher's true spiritual nature, that is, his divine affiliation, but was prevented by a jealous rival who strangled the birds that would have served as part of the divination ritual. And finally, we have also discussed the doubling between Pythagoras and Apollo in Iamblichus's *On the Pythagorean Way of Life.* There are notable differences between Plotinus or Porphyry and Iamblichus in their understandings of this notion. The former two held the position that "our intellect never fully descends from its proper place in the intellectual heights," which means that the "descended intellect enjoys unbroken contact with its undescended counterpart and so can ascend by its own contemplative efforts."[43] In other words, the divine part of ourselves remains connected with highest divinity. Iamblichus, whom Eunapius and presumably Sosipatra followed, insisted "that the intellect descends completely into the body and is cut off from the inner life of universal intellect."[44] However, this does not amount to a denial of our divine double. Rather, Iamblichus "insists on a higher principle residing within us" at the same time as this principle is "fully alien to us." Hence, the "self is profoundly 'self-alienated.'"[45] God-given, divinely sanctioned ritual practices are what aid us in our overcoming this self-alienation. This is because activation of the principle within us must come from outside of us, from the gods themselves.[46] Another way of expressing this is to say that "the gods have given us the ancient prayers with which to activate our alien principle, and so we can become theurgists, that is 'chaperones' or 'cooperators' as the divine meets the divine within us."[47] By relating Sosipatra's prophetic and remote viewing activity, Eunapius is signaling that she has overcome this primordial self-alienation. In other words, this notion of a special form of

43. Stang, *Our Divine Double,* 232.
44. Stang, *Our Divine Double,* 232.
45. Stang, *Our Divine Double,* 232.
46. Stang, *Our Divine Double,* 233.
47. Stang, *Our Divine Double,* 233.

spiritual guardianship between divinities and extraordinary holy people is what helps to explain the miraculous moments in Eunapius's *Lives*. Sosipatra, however, stands out in this regard from many of Eunapius's other subjects in the way her entire biography is suffused with evidence of this divine communion and influence.

There are two more episodes in her story that highlight Sosipatra's extraordinary abilities and her particular blessedness. Both relate to her relationship with her kinsman Philometer. In the first place, he casts a binding spell upon her; in the second, she remotely views an accident he has while driving in a carriage. The story of Philometer's passion for Sosipatra allows readers another fascinating glimpse into the thought world of Late Antiquity. According to Eunapius, Philometer was completely overcome with a romantic obsession for Sosipatra, on account of her "beauty and eloquence." His passion conquered him completely, he "occupied himself with these matters," and as a result, Sosipatra was affected by "his exertions."[48] She revealed her predicament to Maximus, presumably her student at the time, and told him the following: "If Philometer is present, he is just Philometer. . . . But, if I see him departing, my heart inside is stung and in a certain way it is spun outwards."[49] Sosipatra beseeched Maximus to help her with her problem, so painful did she find the situation. As modern readers, who consume an endless supply of entertainment that celebrates romantic passion almost as a virtue, we might wonder why "falling in love" in this manner was so disturbing to Sosipatra, especially because, as we have discussed earlier, she had no qualms about marriage and there were no injunctions among non-Christians against widows taking another partner. So we are perhaps puzzled about why she would seek a remedy for something we think of as a welcome and desirable state of affairs, namely, falling in love, especially given the fact that her feelings are more than reciprocated by Philometer.

Sosipatra's discomfort with excessive passion is not a sign of prudery or of an overly fastidious sexual ethic. She is not like many of her Christian counterparts who eschewed "normal human sexuality," pleasure, and reproduction. She has experienced all of these things without a whiff of ambivalence. Rather, the excessive nature of her feelings causes her to become suspicious that some mischief is afoot given that her feelings

48. Eunap., *VS* 6.82.
49. Eunap., *VS* 6.83–84.

are disproportionate to her present circumstances. Implicit is the notion that Philometer, unlike Eustathius, is not worthy of her, and knowing this himself, he has resorted to ritual, even "magical," measures to capture her affections. It is the excessive nature of her feelings that clues her in. We have plenty of evidence from antiquity that people of all means and social classes resorted to binding spells in their efforts to secure the affections of potential lovers and partners.

Binding "magic" of this sort was tinged with a kind of violence as evidenced by many extant amatory *defixiones* (sexual binding spells) (see Figure 5.3): "Various tablets specify that the object of passion is to be dragged by the hair, deprived of memory and sleep, tormented by passion, and killed with madness." These objects are also striking for their "undisguised sexuality ('join belly to belly, thigh to thigh, black to black,' 'bring her thigh close to his, her genitals close to his in unending intercourse for all the time of her life')."[50]

As part of the remedy for her "love sickness," Sosipatra enlists the help of Maximus to secure her release. Feeling great pride at having been tasked by his teacher with sorting out this tangle, Maximus used his knowledge of sacrifice to discover "what rites Philometer made use of" and worked to counteract them with stronger and more powerful ones.[51]

We might ask why Sosipatra, a powerful holy woman, would need Maximus to help her. After all, when something similar happened to Plotinus, namely, when he felt the violent "magical" attack of a jealous philosophical rival, he was able to turn the attack against its perpetrator just through the power of his own intellect or spirit. One might assume that Eunapius is subtly delimiting the extent of Sosipatra's abilities by relating this episode. On the contrary, I would argue that Eunapius is juxtaposing two kinds or levels of ritual expertise, and in the end, Sosipatra has, in reality, employed a subordinate to engage in a more menial form of ritual activity, one that has a tinge of coercive "magic" to it, one she would rather not stoop to participate in herself. Binding spells were often cast using the help of the spirits of the dead or evil daemons. Hence, casting a counter spell would likely have involved a kind of ritual dirty work.

Sosipatra's superiority to Maximus is affirmed in the final scene of the episode. Upon returning to her after he had completed his work for

50. John G. Gager, *Curse Tablets and Binding Spells from the Ancient World* (New York: Oxford University Press, 1999), 81.

51. Eunap., *VS* 6.85.

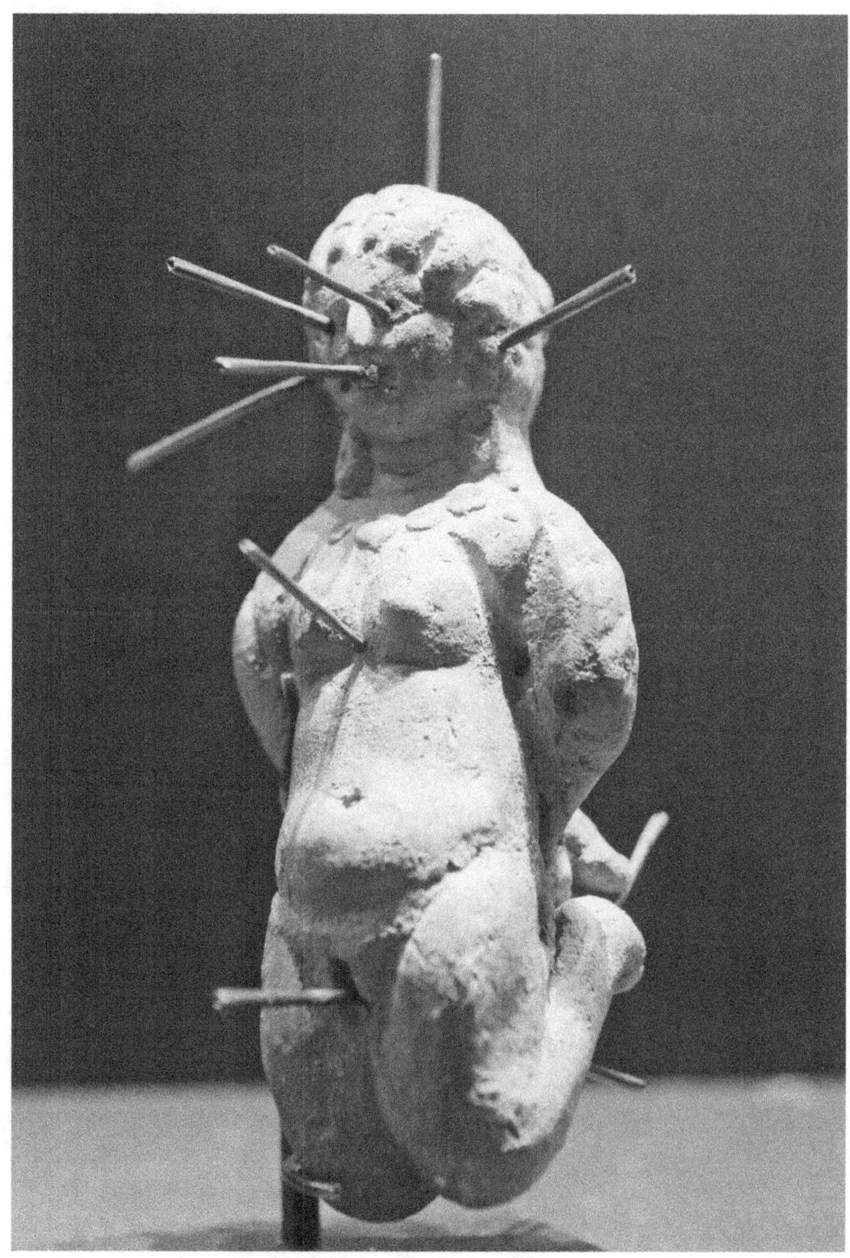

FIGURE 5.3 The "Louvre Doll," figurine used in the context of a binding spell, fourth century CE. Louvre Museum, Paris. Wikimedia Commons.

her, she described to Maximus, as if she had been present, everything he had done on her behalf, including his own prayer and the acts he had performed.[52] At this, Maximus fell in amazement before her, and she took the opportunity to admonish him for tendencies that readers see borne out in other moments in the *Lives*, namely, his hubristic habit of seeking to force the gods to do his will in service to his ambitions. She said to him, "Stand, O child. The gods love you, if you yourself gaze upon them and are not inclined towards earthly goods, which are subject to death."[53] He did not sufficiently heed her words, as we know from these other episodes, but when he met Philometer on his way out from speaking with Sosipatra, he did tell him, "Philometer, friend, stop burning up wood in vain."[54] In other words, Maximus enjoined Philometer to cease to engage in sacrificial activities with a hope of coercing the affections of Sosipatra.

As a result of these events, the relationship between Philometer and Sosipatra returned to one of proper proportion and appropriate regard. Their connection continued to be an important one for her, however, as she broke off one day in a lecture on the immortality of the soul to inform her audience of another "remote viewing" she was experiencing, this time of Philometer's carriage overturning and of the severe but non-fatal injuries that he sustained as a result.[55]

All of these stories about Sosipatra's wonder working and oracular activities form part of an argument Eunapius makes in the *Lives* about the best form of life for the theurgically inclined philosopher primarily in his own time, and not necessarily in the time when his subjects actually lived. Eunapius was writing his account at the end of the fourth century when there was far less tolerance for polytheistic forms of ritual engagement. In order to understand more fully the crux of his argument, it is important to identify the competing alternatives he was seeking to discredit in one way or other. One of these is certainly various forms of Christianity. The other, however, is the ritual of overly enthusiastic theurgists who from an outsiders' perspective may in fact look more like "magicians" than ritually oriented philosophers. Theurgists of this bent,

52. Eunap., *VS* 6.86.
53. Eunap., *VS* 6.86.
54. Eunap., *VS* 6.87–88.
55. Eunap., *VS* 6.89–93.

such as Maximus of Ephesus, brought unwanted attention and censure on the philosophical circles Eunapius both narrates and inhabits.[56]

As a number of scholars have noted, Eunapius is subtly critical of Christianity—subtly because of the political climate at the end of the fourth century when he was writing. For instance, his description of Sosipatra's son, Antoninus, serves as a foil to the Christian monks of Egypt.[57] The image of Sosipatra is also a powerful counterpoint to the kinds of ideal images biographers of Christian women were producing, especially for women of the same social class. Although we might emphasize similarities between the portrayals of Sosipatra and women such as Macrina, Eunapius is more likely trying to distinguish Sosipatra from her Christian counterparts. Indeed, he may have felt compelled to include her in his collective biography precisely because so many Christian men were writing so enthusiastically about ascetic women such as Macrina, the Melanias, and Syncletica, and casting them in the role of teachers and spiritual guides.[58]

We might ask then exactly how Sosipatra departs from the Christian ideal in Eunapius's narrative. First, she actually receives an education. Although her teachers turn out to be something akin to *daemones*, this in fact signals the superiority of her education over her male peers. Hence, unlike Christian holy women, Sosipatra was supremely educated in traditional Greek *paideia* (recall that she has ever on her lips the works of the poets, philosophers, and orators) via a process that represented the pinnacle of philosophical formation. In this respect, she is quite unlike Macrina and other Christian women whom hagiographers cast as teachers entirely uneducated in Greek philosophy and literature. For instance, Macrina, according to her brother, happened upon tenets of a "modified Origenism" merely via the processes of reading scripture and contemplating.[59]

My argument is that Eunapius does not so much differentiate Sosipatra's education from that of the men who populate his biography

---

56. Nicola Denzey Lewis, "Living Images of the Divine: Female Theurgists in Late Antiquity," in *Daughters of Hecate: Women and Magic in the Ancient World*, ed. Dayna S. Kalleres and Kimberly B. Stratton (Oxford: Oxford University Press, 2014), 274–97.

57. Arthur P. Urbano, *The Philosophical Life: Biography and the Crafting of Intellectual Identity in Late Antiquity*, Patristic Monograph Series, vol. 21 (Washington, DC: Catholic University of America Press, 2013), 270.

58. Elizabeth A. Clark, "The Lady Vanishes: Dilemmas of a Feminist Historian after the 'Linguistic Turn,'" *Church History* 67, no. 1 (1998): 1–31.

59. Clark, "The Lady Vanishes," 27.

as place it on a continuum where it represents a kind of *eidos*, the ideal form of divine education of the soul to which the Iamblichean lineage aspired. In other words, "her education in philosophy and theurgy by the gods and *daimones*, the cause and goal of Iamblichean philosophical, intellectual, and ritual practice, affirmed the conventional institutional paths by which [Eunapius's] male subjects pursued the same goal."[60]

Eunapius further distinguished Sosipatra from Christian women by highlighting her participation in marriage, childbearing and child-rearing, and family life. On his account, she also did not participate in any form of ascetic self-discipline. What she did do, unabashedly, was teach male students in her own philosophical school in Pergamum after the death of her husband. In my estimation, Eunapius casts Sosipatra as a superior sort of philosophical teacher, in terms of both her formation and her pedagogy, in part to present readers with a contrastive image to the one being constructed by Christian hagiographers of female saints.[61]

The second role Sosiptra plays is to critique the ritual excesses of some theurgists, excesses that had in the past brought censure by Christian authorities. For instance, as we have repeatedly seen, Maximus of Ephesus is an ambivalent figure in Eunapius's narrative overall. Although he often sings Maximus's praises and reminisces fondly about the golden days of Julian's ascension, Eunapius juxtaposes Maximus's philosophical and theurgical tendencies with those of at least three figures: Maximus's wife, his own teacher Chrysanthius, and of course, Sosipatra.

Eunapius describes Maximus's wife thus: "So profound was her knowledge of philosophy that she made Maximus seem not to know how to swim or even to know his alphabet."[62] And we have already discussed the different responses to the negative oracle on the part of Chrysanthius and Maximus. We have also seen how Eunapius situates Maximus as Sosipatra's subordinate in the episode with Philometer.

Although Eunapius is generally in favor of a theurgical interpretation of the Platonic lineage, he uses a number of episodes and figures such as Sosipatra and Antoninus, both of whom are receptive to the gods but do not actively seek to manipulate cosmic forces, in order

60. Urbano, *The Philosophical Life*, 258.

61. As Averil Cameron notes: "Christian and Neoplatonic rivalries could seem to be expressing themselves in a war of biography." Averil Cameron, *Christianity and the Rhetoric of Empire: The Development of Christian Discourse* (Berkeley: University of California Press, 1991), 145.

62. Eunap., *VS* 7.43 (trans. Wright, 443).

to domesticate theurgy and to lop off its more problematic branches, namely, those that might lead its adherents too far into the realm of what some might call "coercive magic." This domestication is also seen in Sosipatra's interactions with Maximus around the binding spell cast by Philometer. In other words, it is a moment when Eunapius signals her true superiority by juxtaposing the kind of *techne* involved in binding and releasing with the real work of the divinization of the soul.

In sum, Eunapius uses Sosipatra to consolidate an understanding of not only late Roman Platonism as theurgy but also as a particular kind of theurgy. His ideal, which maps onto political and religious realities of the late fourth century, is one that avoids hubris by working with the sympathetic connections built into the cosmos at the time of its creation and emphasizes the purification and divinization of the soul in anticipation of communication and blessing from the supralunary realms where truly pure and holy souls may ascend after they leave this world. He de-emphasizes theurgy as *techne* in favor of theurgy as oracular and prophetic activity. Sosipatra and her son Antoninus are exemplary of this kind of theurgy.

6

Conclusion

In drawing to a close our study of the remarkable, albeit highly fictional, figure of Sosipatra of Pergamum, it is important to draw to attention to some of the broader implications of her life for our understanding of women and society in Late Antiquity. We clearly see, especially when we compare her life with that of wealthy Christian women such as Melania the Younger or Olympias, that resources and social standing were determining factors in what a woman was allowed to do with her life in the ancient world. Even so, by the time Eunapius is writing in the late fourth century, the situation is beginning to change in a way that increasingly circumscribes opportunities for even wealthy women in terms of their engagement in intellectual culture, pedagogical activities, and leadership. For instance, although Sosipatra subscribed to and taught in the ritually inflected Platonic tradition of Iamblichus, a tradition that would have been far more threatening to Christians based on its emphasis on traditional polytheistic beliefs and rituals than many other philosophical schools of the time, she was never subject to the violence that ended the life of Hypatia of Alexandria, a Platonist who clearly eschewed Iamblichan philosophy. Christians would have found Sosipatra's strain of Platonism more problematic because of its deep engagement with and justification of polytheistic forms of ritual and worship. Hypatia seems to have subscribed to a more henotheistic or monotheistic form of Platonism. Nonetheless, some Christian leaders such as Cyril the Bishop of Alexandria, saw her as wielding too much influence on some of the city's most important politicians, in particular, the governor Orestes.[1] The late fourth and early fifth centuries witnessed

---

1. Edward Jay Watts, *Hypatia: The Life and Legend of an Ancient Philosopher*, Women in Antiquity (New York: Oxford University Press, 2017), 113–17.

Sosipatra of Pergamum. Heidi Marx, Oxford University Press (2021). © Oxford University Press.
DOI: 10.1093/oso/9780190618858.003.0006

trends such as the consolidation of and increased hegemony of clerical authority (especially that of bishops), theological disputes polarizing Christian populations around the Mediterranean that were frequently accompanied by violence, the rise of anti-Jewish polemic (which also often ended in violence, as we also see in Cyril's Alexandria), and so forth. These trends affected traditional polytheists, Jews, and heterodox Christians alike. For instance, this time period saw the end of "eso-teric" Christian instruction, the end of the "tradition of the Christian gnōstikos, the end of a form of life among early Christian groups that had begun in the second century."[2] In terms of diversity of student pop-ulation, boldness of theological and philosophical speculation, and communal life, the school of Origen at Alexandria likely had more in common with the school of Plotinus at Rome than with later iterations of the Alexandrian catechetical school.

In my book, *Spiritual Taxonomies and Ritual Authority: Platonists, Priests, and Gnostics in the Third Century* C.E., I note the many intellec-tually rich and productive conversations and debates that figures such as Plotinus, Origen, Porphyry, Iamblichus, and certain "gnostics" were having across what we might inadequately call "confessional" lines. But a century and a half later, things were changing. While Eunapius used his image of Sosipatra to recall and mourn the golden days of the Iamblichan past, we see a similar shift in Christian intellectual cul-ture away from more esoteric and experimental forms of Christianity. Shortly after Eunapius's lifetime, the Academy in Athens closed and the-urgical Platonism "went underground" until the Renaissance, except where it found a brief kind of re-expression in the work of a figure such as Pseudo-Dionysus the Areopagite.[3] Female philosophy teachers such as Sosipatra or Hypatia became even rarer in subsequent centuries. We have to wait for a figure such as Hildegard of Bingen in the twelfth cen-tury before we encounter a record of a similarly polymathic woman. This is not to say they did not exist; we simply do not get to read about them in written records. Sosipatra's story evokes a whole world, one very different from our own. Her tale is embedded in a cosmos very foreign to us today, one where five-year-old girls can be taught by the incarnate

2. Robin Darling Young, "A Life in Letters," in *Melania: Early Christianity through the Life of One Family*, ed. C. M. Chin and Caroline T. Schroeder, Christianity in Late Antiquity (Oakland: University of California Press, 2017), 166.

3. Gregory Shaw, "Neoplatonic Theurgy and Dionysius the Areopagite," *Journal of Early Christian Studies* 7, no. 4 (1999): 573–99.

souls of celestial beings, one where the gods communicate with particularly holy men and women, one where macro- and microcosmic connections can be activated to make someone fall madly in love or levitate or animate statues. It is a world very different from our own, but entering it forces us to rethink our assumptions about gender roles in antiquity and engage in more subtle readings of our sources. I have grown quite fond of Sosipatra in writing this account of her legendary life. She is, of course, a figment of Eunapius's imagination in many important respects, and so also now a figment of mine. But I have enjoyed immensely trying to imagine her life at the same time that I have had to let go of any dogmatic attempt to ground it in the reality of fourth-century Asia Minor. She will remain for me elusive and evocative. And that is as it should be.

APPENDIX

Translation of Passages Relating to Sosipatra in Eunapius's Lives of the Philosophers and Sophists (6. 53–96)

The following is a translation of the passages in Eunapius in which he tells the story of Sosipatra's life. This section of the *Lives* starts as a kind of digression from his account of her husband Eustathius. But Eunapius spends far more time discussing Sosipatra's life and activities than almost all other subjects in his work.[1]

53. Well then, the great Eustathius married Sosipatra, who proved through the superiority of her wisdom that her husband was like cheap and trivial merchandise. **54.** His wife's fame spread so extensively, that this woman deserves to be spoken of at greater length and in catalogues of wise men. She was from Asia, near Ephesus. The river Cayster, which travels close and then flows through that expanse of land, gives its name to the plain. Her family was blessed and wealthy, just as her forefathers had been. There was so great a quality of beauty and virtue shining down upon her infancy, that, even before she could talk, she made everything more valuable. **55.** Sosipatra was starting her fifth year, when two old men advanced upon one of the estates of her parents. One was further advanced in age, but both past their prime; they had copious wallets and

1. Robert Nau, the translator, has used the critical edition by Richard Goulet as the basis for his translation of these passages: Eunapius, *Vies de philosophes et de sophistes*, Collection des universités de France. Série grecque, 508 (Paris: Les Belles Lettres, 2014).

wore skins on their backs. They convinced the overseer—it was easy for them to do this—to commit the care of the newly sprouting vines to them. **56**. When the harvest turned out to be beyond expectation—the owner was present and Sosipatra was present too—there was endless wonder and the marvel hinted at the possibility of some divinatory intervention. **57**. The estate owner made them his dinner guests and paid them especial attention; at the same time he strongly rebuked their fellow fieldhands for not accomplishing what they had. **58**. The old men won Greek hospitality and dinner, and they were stung deeply and conquered by the beauty and forwardness of the little child Sosipatra. They said: "For our part, we do keep the rest of our gifts to ourselves, hidden and secret, but in regard to the abundance arising from our favor, which you applaud, that is a laughing matter or a game, a sort of trivializing of things that are magnified in our hands. **59**. If you wish for some repayment from us for yourself equal in value to this dinner and your acts of hospitality, and a payment not in money nor in perishable and corrupted favors, but one on a higher level than you and your life, a gift that reaches the heavens and extends to the stars, give this Sosipatra to us who are in a truer sense nourishers and parents. For five years, have no fears about sickness or death afflicting the young girl, but be at ease and steadfast. **60**. Be careful, though, not to tread on this estate until, under the circling solar cycles, the fifth year comes. In addition, your wealth will burgeon and sprout anew spontaneously from the land, and not only will your daughter not be like a woman or a human being, but also you yourself will apprehend something greater in the girl. And so, if you have a noble heart, accept the things said with upturned hands; but if you vacillate amidst any suspicions, let nothing have been said by us." **61**. Faced with these things, her father bit his tongue, and cowering in fear he handed off and surrendered the child into their care. He then summoned his estate manager and said to him: "Furnish generously as much as the old men want and ask no questions." **62**. He said these things. Before the break of dawn, he set out as if running away from his daughter and the estate too. **63**. And they—whether they were heroes, or spirits, or a race in some way more divine—undertook the child's care and not one person knew into what mysteries they inducted her and it was obscure even to those who really wanted to know what purpose they had in mind for making her divine. **64**. Now the deadline was approaching and it coincided with all other matters regarding the revenues of the estate. The girl's father was on the farm. He didn't recognize the girl's stature and she seemed to have a different sort of beauty. **65.** The child hardly knew her father. Further, he greeted her with reverence—he so seemed to look upon another woman. When her teachers were present and the table was set, they said: "Ask the maiden whatever you wish." **66.** But she interjected: "Rather ask instead, father, what happened to you on the road." He left it to her to answer—because of his good fortune, he rode in a four-wheeled carriage and many calamities happen with such carriages—and she related everything, voices, threats, fears, just as if she had been holding the reins with him. **67.** Her father reached such a pitch of amazement that he passed from amazement to being awestruck and convinced that his daughter was a goddess. He prostrated himself before the men and beseeched them to say who they were. Only with difficulty and slowly—perhaps it was also decreed so by a god—did they reveal that they were not uninitiated in the wisdom called Chaldean, and they only revealed this through dark sayings and while bowing their heads. **68.** And so, Sosipatra's father, having prostrated himself before the men, while clasping their knees, beseeched them to be the masters of his estate, to keep the child under their power, and to initiate her in the higher mystery. They had stopped speaking, but they nodded in assent that they would do so. He took heart and at the same time was mystified by the event, just as if he had attained some promise or oracular response. **69.** He filled his soul with the praise of Homer for celebrating in song just such an extraordinary and divine event:

> And the gods, like unto strangers of foreign land,
> being in all shapes, do frequent cities.[2]

For truly he really did imagine that he had met with foreign men who were also gods. **70.** After he had his fill of the matter, her father was overpowered by sleep; but the men retired from dinner and had the girl accompany them. With considerable kindness and earnest zeal, they handed over to her the array of the clothing in which she had been initiated. Likewise, they set forth certain other instruments and ordered that she seal her chest—also having cast into Sosipatra's chest some small books. **71.** She rejoiced in the men no less than her father had. When dawn appeared, the doors were opened, the men proceeded to their labors, and the old men, as was their wont, went out with them. The girl ran to her father bearing good news and one of her servants was

---

2. Hom., *Odyssey* xvii.485.

bringing her chest. **72.** After he asked for the money he had with him for the needs that arose, and asked the managers for all they had for expenses, and sent for the men, but they were nowhere to be seen. He said to Sosipatra: "What does this mean, child?" **73.** She paused a little, then said: "Well now I fully see what had been said. You see, when they passed on these things in tears to me they said: 'Look after them, o child, for we, having been carried to the Western Ocean, will return in no time.'" This demonstrated very clearly that those who had appeared were *daemones*. **74.** They left intending to depart to wherever they departed. Her father, having received a child who had been made divine and who, though with a sound mind, was possessed of a god, let her live how she wished and he didn't trouble himself at all over her affairs, except for how much he was vexed by her silence. **75.** While she came into the full bloom of her youth, she did not have other teachers, and yet she had on her lips the books of the poets, philosophers, and orators. That woman explained with careless ease, as she painlessly assailed the truth, whatever points others, amidst labor and hard work, could only just begin barely and indistinctly to understand. **76.** Well then, she decided to wed. It was indisputable that Eustathius alone of all men was worthy of marriage to her. She addressed Eustathius, and the others present, saying: "But listen now, Eustathius, and let those present be witnesses: I will bear three children by you and all will attain success in what is considered noble for mankind, but only one in what is considered noble for gods. **77.** Further, you yourself will pass away ahead of me and be allotted a fair and fitting lot, but I myself perhaps a higher one. For in your case, you will traverse the region below the moon with a good and smooth passage. You will serve and philosophize no longer than the fifth year; for so does your phantom say to me. But, mind you, you will arrive at the region under the moon with its noble and marshalled course. **78.** I also wanted to speak about my affairs . . ." She paused her statement briefly and then shouted out: "but my god forbids me!" **79.** Having said these things—for the Fates were in agreement—she married Eustathius and the things which she had spoken differed in no way from unshakable oracular responses, for all the things happened and turned out just as they were said. **80.** In the case of Sosipatra, it would be necessary to add the following to the above incidents. Sosipatra, after Eustasthius passed away, returned to her former properties and was passing her time in Asia and ancient Pergamum. The great Aedesius treated her with affection, provided for her, and he was educating her sons. **81.** Sosipatra competed with him as she philosophized in her own house. After students gathered at Aedesius's, they then had recourse to that woman as a teacher, and there was no one who did not greatly love and admire the accuracy of Aedesius in what he said, and did not adore and revere the divine inspiration of the woman. **82.** And so Philometor, one of her cousins, came to desire her. He had been overcome by her beauty and her words, and also had recognized that the woman was in some way divine. Lust compelled him, and he was overpowered. He occupied himself with these matters and the woman did feel something from his exertions. To Maximus—this man positioned himself at the fore of Aedesius's crowd and he wasn't from a different family—she said: **83.** "Well, Maximus, that I be free from difficulties, please find out about the suffering that afflicts me." He replied: "Well, what suffering is this?" and she said to him: "If Philometor is present, he is just Philometor; he does not differ one iota from the majority of us. **84.** But, if I see him departing, my heart inside is stung and in a certain way, as if tortured, is twisted outwards." She added: "But see to it that you contend on my behalf and show that you are favored by the gods." After he heard this, Maximus departed. He was swollen with pride, as if he already shared the company of the gods, seeing that so great a woman entrusted to him matters of such importance. **85.** Philometor continued with the plans he had set in place and Maximus continually countered them. Maximus had learned well through his knowledge of sacrifice what rites Philometor made use of, and he put an end to his weaker rites by a stronger and more powerful one. Once he had finished, Maximus ran to Sosipatra and required that she keep a close watch over whether she suffered the same thing in the future. **86.** She, though, declared that she no longer suffered and then gave an account to Maximus of his prayer and every act. She also revealed the hour, as if being there too, at which he was doing these things, and she revealed the signs that appeared. With mouth agape, he fell to the ground and confessed openly that Sosipatra was a goddess. In response to this, she said: "Stand, o child. The gods love you, if you yourself gaze upon them and are not inclined towards earthly goods, which are subject to death." **87.** After he had heard these things, he went off, and he was even more prideful now, since he had experienced with certainty the woman's divinity. A cheerful Philometor, who was coming in with his many companions, ran into him near the door as he left. **88.** Maximus shouted to him from afar and said: "Philometor, friend, stop burning up wood in vain," having seen perhaps something of the sort regarding what Philometor mischievously had been doing. **89**. As a result, he treated Maximus with utmost respect and considered him a god. He put a stop to his plan and made light of the fact that he had even undertaken the endeavor. For the rest of time, Sosipatra viewed Philometor differently and realistically, admiring him, in that he admired her. **90**. At any rate, on one occasion when everyone had gathered together at her house—Philemetor, mind you, was not present, but he was spending time in the country—a proposition had been made and the theme and the inquiry were about the soul. **91**. This set in motion much discussion. Sosipatra started to speak. Little by little through her proofs, she did away with what the others proposed and next fell into an account about the soul's journey down and about what is punished and what is immortal. In the middle of her Corybantic frenzy and Bacchic inspiration, just as if she had altogether lost her speech, she grew silent and after letting a little time pass she shouted out into their midst: "What is this? My relative Philometor rides a carriage, and the carriage has been overturned, and that man's legs are in peril. **92**. But, his servants have extricated him safe and sound, except for the wounds he has received to his elbows and knees, which in fact pose no danger. He groans away while borne on a litter." **93**. She said these things and they turned out to be true. Everyone knew that Sosipatra was everywhere and that she was present at everything that happened, just as the philosophers claim about the gods. **94**. She died after the three children. I need not record the names of two of these, but Antoninus was worthy of his forefathers. He dwelled at the Canobic mouth of the Nile and having dedicated himself wholly to the hallowed things there, he spent his strength on the prophecies of his mother. **95**. The young men who had healthy souls and had set their hearts on philosophy would flock to him, and so the temple was filled with young men who were its priests. **96**. While he himself still seemed to be human and associated with humans, he would prophesize to his associates that after his time the temple would no longer be, but the great and sacred temples of Serapis would pass on and be changed into that which is dark looking and misshapen, and a fantastic and unsightly darkness would tyrannize the most beautiful things on earth. Time vindicated everything and indeed this matter came to have the power of an oracle.

Bibliography

Ancient Sources: Editions and Translations

Chaldaean Oracles

Majercik, Ruth Dorothy. *The Chaldean Oracles: Text, Translation, and Commentary.* Leiden: Brill, 1989.

Eunapius

Goulet, Richard. *Eunapius. Vies de philosophes et de sophistes.* Collection des universités de France. Série grecque, 508. Paris: Les Belles Lettres, 2014.

Wright, Wilmer Cave. *Philostratus and Eunapius: The Lives of the Sophists.* Cambridge, MA: Harvard University Press, 1989.

Iamblichus

Dillon, John, and Jackson P. Hershbell. *Iamblichus: On the Pythagorean Way of Life.* Society of Biblical Literature, Texts and Translations 29. Atlanta: Scholars Press, 1991.

Iamblichus. *On the Mysteries.* Translated Emma C. Clarke, John M. Dillon, and Jackson P. Hershbell. Atlanta: Society of Biblical Literature, 2003.

Plotinus

Plotinus. *Enneads.* Translated by A. H. Armstrong. 7 vols. Cambridge, MA: Harvard University Press, 1978–1988.

Plotinus. *Plotinus: The Enneads.* Translated by Stephen MacKenna. London: Penguin Books, 1991.

Porphyry

Porphyry. *On Abstinence from Killing Animals*. Translated by Gillian Clark. Ithaca, NY: Cornell University Press, 2000.

Wilberding, James. *Porphyry: To Gaurus on How Embryos Are Ensouled and On What Is in Our Power*. London: Bristol Classical Press, 2011.

Pre-Socratic Philosophers

Kirk, G. S., J. E. Raven, and Malcolm Schofield. *The Presocratic Philosophers: A Critical History with a Selection of Texts*. 2nd ed. Cambridge: Cambridge University Press, 1983.

Modern Sources

Addey, Crystal. *Divination and Theurgy in Neoplatonism: Oracles of the Gods*. Ashgate Studies in Philosophy and Theology in Late Antiquity. Burlington, VT: Routledge, 2014.

Alberici, Lisa A., and Mary Harlow. "Age and Innocence: Female Transitions to Adulthood in Late Antiquity." *Hesperia Supplements* 41 (2007): 193–203.

Athanassiadi, Polymnia. "The Chaldaean Oracles: Theology and Theurgy." In *Pagan Monotheism in Late Antiquity*, edited by Polymnia Athanassiadi and Michael Frede, 149–84. Oxford: Clarendon Press, 1999.

Athanassiadi, Polymnia. "The Divine Man of Late Hellenism: A Sociable and Popular Figure." In *Divine Men and Women in the History and Society of Late Hellenism*, edited by Maria Dzielska and Kamilla Twardowska, 13–28. Krakow, Poland: Jagiellonian University Press, 2013.

Banchich, Thomas M. "On Goulet's Chronology of Eunapius' Life and Works." *Journal of Hellenic Studies* 107 (1987): 164–67.

Banchich, Thomas M. "Eunapius in Athens." *Phoenix* 50, no. 3/4 (1996): 304–11.

Banchich, Thomas M. "The Date of Eunapius' Vitae Sophistarum." *Greek, Roman, and Byzantine Studies* 25, no. 2 (2004): 183–92.

Barrier, Jeremy W. *The Acts of Paul and Thecla: A Critical Introduction and Commentary*. Tübingen: Mohr Siebeck, 2009.

Boedeker, Deborah. "Family Matters: Domestic Religion in Classical Greece." In *Household and Family Religion in Antiquity*, edited by John Bodel and Saul M. Olyan, 229–47. Malden, MA: Wiley-Blackwell, 2009.

Bowes, Kimberly Diane. *Houses and Society in the Later Roman Empire*. Duckworth Debates in Archaeology. London: Duckworth, 2010.

Bradley, Keith. *Discovering the Roman Family: Studies in Roman Social History*. New York: Oxford University Press, 1991.

Bradley, Keith. "Images of Childhood in Classical Antiquity." In *The Routledge History of Childhood in the Western World*, edited by Paula S. Fass, 17–38. London: Routledge, 2013.

Brøns, Cecilie. *Gods and Garments: Textiles in Greek Sanctuaries in the 7th–1st Centuries BC*. Oxford: Oxbow Books, 2016.

Brown, Peter. "The Rise and Function of the Holy Man in Late Antiquity." *Journal of Roman Studies* 61 (1971): 80–101.

Brown, Peter. "The Philosopher and Society in Late Antiquity." In *The Philosopher and Society in Late Antiquity: Protocol of the Thirty-Fourth Colloquy, 3 December 1978*, edited by Edward C. Hobbs and Wilhelm Wuellner, 1–17. Berkeley, CA: Center for Hermeneutical Studies in Hellenistic and Modern Culture, 1980.

Brown, Peter. *Power and Persuasion in Late Antiquity: Towards a Christian Empire*. Madison: University of Wisconsin Press, 1992.

Burrus, Virginia. *The Sex Lives of the Saints: An Erotics of Ancient Hagiography*. Philadelphia: University of Pennsylvania Press, 2004.

Butler, Judith. *Gender Trouble: Feminism and the Subversion of Identity*. Thinking Gender. New York: Routledge, 1990.

Caldwell, Lauren E. *Roman Girlhood and the Fashioning of Femininity*. Cambridge: Cambridge University Press, 2015.

Cameron, Averil. *Christianity and the Rhetoric of Empire: The Development of Christian Discourse*. Berkeley: University of California Press, 1991.

Carroll, Maureen. "Archaeological and Epigraphic Evidence for Infancy in the Roman World." In *Oxford Handbook of the Archaeology of Childhood*, edited by Sally Crawford, Dawn M. Hadley, and Gillian Shepherd, 148–64. Oxford: Oxford University Press, 2018.

Chin, C. M. "Cosmos." In *Late Ancient Knowing: Explorations in Intellectual History*, edited by C. M. Chin and Moulie Vidas, 99–116. Berkeley: University of California Press, 2015.

Chin, C. M., and Moulie Vidas, eds. *Late Ancient Knowing: Explorations in Intellectual History*. Oakland: University of California Press, 2015.

Clark, Elizabeth A. *The Life of Melania the Younger: Introduction, Translation, and Commentary*. New York: Edwin Mellon Press, 1984.

Clark, Elizabeth A. "The Lady Vanishes: Dilemmas of a Feminist Historian after the 'Linguistic Turn.'" *Church History* 67, no. 1 (1998): 1–31.

Clark, Gillian. *Women in Late Antiquity: Pagan and Christian Life-Styles*. Oxford: Clarendon Press, 1993.

Clark, Gillian. *Monica: An Ordinary Saint*. Women in Antiquity. New York: Oxford University Press, 2015.

Cox Miller, Patricia. *Biography in Late Antiquity: A Quest for the Holy Man*. Transformation of the Classical Heritage, 5. Berkeley: University of California Press, 1983.

Cox Miller, Patricia. "Strategies of Representation in Collective Biography: Constructing the Subject as Holy." In *Greek Biography and Panegyric in Late Antiquity*, edited by Tomas Hägg and Philip Rousseau, 209–54. Transformation of the Classical Heritage. Berkeley: University of California Press, 2000.

Cox Miller, Patricia. "Is There a Harlot in This Text? Hagiography and the Grotesque," *Journal of Medieval and Early Modern Studies* 33, no. 3 (2003): 419–35.

Cribiore, Raffaella. *Gymnastics of the Mind: Greek Education in Hellenistic and Roman Egypt*. Princeton, NJ: Princeton University Press, 2001.

Cribiore, Raffaella. *The School of Libanius in Late Antique Antioch*. Princeton, NJ: Princeton University Press, 2007.

Darling Young, Robin. "A Life in Letters." In *Melania: Early Christianity through the Life of One Family*, edited by C. M. Chin and Caroline T. Schroeder, 153–70. Christianity in Late Antiquity. Oakland: University of California Press, 2017.

Dasen, Véronique. "Childbirth and Infancy in Greek and Roman Antiquity." In *A Companion to Families in the Greek and Roman Worlds*, edited by Beryl Rawson, 291–314. Blackwell Companions to the Ancient World. Literature and Culture. Malden, MA: Wiley-Blackwell, 2011.

Davis, Stephen J. *The Cult of St. Thecla: A Tradition of Women's Piety in Late Antiquity*. Oxford: Oxford University Press, 2001.

Denzey Lewis, Nicola. "Living Images of the Divine: Female Theurgists in Late Antiquity." In *Daughters of Hecate: Women and Magic in the Ancient World*, edited by Dayna S. Kalleres and Kimberly B. Stratton, 274–97. Oxford: Oxford University Press, 2014.

Digeser, Elizabeth DePalma. *A Threat to Public Piety: Christians, Platonists, and the Great Persecution*. Ithaca, NY: Cornell University Press, 2012.

Dillon, John. "Iamblichus of Chalcis (c. 240–325 AD)." *Aufstieg Und Niedergang Der Römischen Welt* 2, no. 36 (1987): 862–909.

Dixon, Suzanne. *The Roman Mother*. Norman: University of Oklahoma Press, 1988.

Dixon, Suzanne. *The Roman Family*. Ancient Society and History. Baltimore: Johns Hopkins University Press, 1992.

Dixon, Suzanne. *Childhood, Class, and Kin in the Roman World*. London: Routledge, 2001.

Dodds, E. R. *The Greeks and the Irrational*. Berkeley: University of California Press, 1951.

Dodds, E. R. *Pagan and Christian in an Age of Anxiety: Some Aspects of Religious Experience from Marcus Aurelius to Constantine*. Cambridge: Cambridge University Press, 1965.

Doerfler, Maria. "Holy Households." In *Melania: Early Christianity through the Life of One Family*, edited by C. M. Chin and Caroline T. Schroeder, 71–85. Berkeley: University of California Press, 2016.

Dzielska, Maria, and Kamilla Twardowska, eds. *Divine Men and Women in the History and Society of Late Hellenism*. Krakow, Poland: Jagiellonian University Press, 2013.

Elm, Susanna. *Sons of Hellenism, Fathers of the Church Emperor Julian, Gregory of Nazianzus, and the Vision of Rome*. Transformation of the Classical Heritage 49. Berkeley: University of California Press, 2012.

Eshleman, Kendra. *The Social World of Intellectuals in the Roman Empire: Sophists, Philosophers, and Christians*. Greek Culture in the Roman World. Cambridge: Cambridge University Press, 2012.

Evans Grubbs, Judith. *Law and Family in Late Antiquity: The Emperor Constantine's Marriage Legislation*. Oxford: Clarendon Press, 1995.

Evans Grubbs, Judith. *The Oxford Handbook of Childhood and Education in the Classical World/Parkin, Tim G*. Oxford Handbooks. Oxford: Oxford University Press, 2013.

Fass, Paula S. *The Routledge History of Childhood in the Western World*. Routledge Histories. London: Routledge, 2013.

Finamore, John F. "Iamblichus on the Grades of Virtue." In *Iamblichus and the Foundations of Late Platonism*, edited by E.V. Afonasin, John M. Dillon, and John F. Finamore, 113–32. Leiden: Brill, 2012.

Fowden, Garth. "The Platonist Philosopher and His Circle in Late Antiquity." *Philosophia* 7 (1977): 359–83.

Fowden, Garth. "The Pagan Holy Man in Late Antique Society." *Journal of Hellenic Studies* 102 (1982): 33–59.

Frankfurter, David. "The Consequences of Hellenism in Late Antique Egypt: Religious Worlds and Actors." *Archiv Für Religionsgeschichte* 2, no. 2 (2010): 162–94.

Gager, John G. *Curse Tablets and Binding Spells from the Ancient World*. New York: Oxford University Press, 1999.

Goulet, Richard. "Sur la chronologie de la vie et des oeuvres d'Eunape de Sardes." *Journal of Hellenic Studies* 100 (1980): 60–72.

Graf, Fritz. *Roman Festivals in the Greek East: From the Early Empire to the Middle Byzantine Era*. Cambridge: Cambridge University Press, 2015.

Hadot, Pierre. *Philosophy as a Way of Life: Spiritual Exercises from Socrates to Foucault*. Malden, MA: Blackwell, 1995.

Hadot, Pierre. *The Inner Citadel: The Meditations of Marcus Aurelius*. Cambridge, MA: Harvard University Press, 1998.

Harich-Schwarzbauer, Henriette. "Das Seelengefährt in Der Lehre Der Theurgin Sosipatra (Eunapios VPS 466,5,1-471,9,17)." *Archaiognosia*. Supplement 8 (2009): 61–71.

Hersch, Karen K. *The Roman Wedding: Ritual and Meaning in Antiquity*. Cambridge: Cambridge University Press, 2010.

Johnson, Aaron. *Religion and Identity in Porphyry of Tyre*. Cambridge: Cambridge University Press, 2013.

Johnston, Sarah Iles. *Hekate Soteira: A Study of Hekate's Role in the Chaldean Oracles and Related Literature*. American Classical Studies 21. Atlanta: Scholars Press, 1990.

Johnston, Sarah Iles. "Working Overtime in the Afterlife; or, No Rest for the Virtuous." In *Heavenly Realms and Earthly Realities in Late Antique Religions*, edited by Annette Yoshiko Reed and Ra'anan S. Boustan, 85–100. Cambridge: Cambridge University Press, 2004.

Kaufmann-Heinimann, Annemarie. "Religion in the House." In *A Companion to Roman Religion*, edited by Jörg Rüpke, 188–201. Malden, MA: Blackwell, 2011.

Koester, Helmut, and Harvard Divinity School. *Ephesos, Metropolis of Asia: An Interdisciplinary Approach to Its Archaeology, Religion, and Culture/Edited by Helmut Koester*. Harvard Theological Studies, No. 41. Cambridge, MA: Distributed by Harvard University Press for Harvard Theological Studies/Harvard Divinity School, 2004.

Kraemer, Ross Shepherd, and Mary Rose D'Angelo, eds. *Women and Christian Origins*. Oxford: Oxford University Press, 1999.

Kuefler, Mathew. "The Marriage Revolution in Late Antiquity: The Theodosian Code and Later Roman Marriage Law." *Journal of Family History* 32, no. 4 (October 1, 2007): 343–70.

Laes, Christian. *Children in the Roman Empire: Outsiders Within*. Cambridge: Cambridge University Press, 2011.

LaFosse, Mona Tokarek. "Age Hierarchy and Social Networks among Urban Women in the Roman East." In *Mediterranean Families in Antiquity: Households, Extended Families, and Domestic Space*, edited by Sabine R. Huebner and Geoffrey S. Nathan, 204–20. Chichester, West Sussex: Wiley Blackwell, 2017.

Lewis, Mary E. *The Bioarchaeology of Children: Perspectives from Biological and Forensic Anthropology*. Cambridge: Cambridge University Press, 2007.

Lewis, Mary E. "Diseases and Trauma in the Children from Roman Britain." In *Oxford Handbook of the Archaeology of Childhood*, edited by Sally Crawford, Dawn M. Hadley, and Gillian Shepherd, 467–82. Oxford: Oxford University Press, 2018.

Maguire, Henry. "The Good Life." In *Late Antiquity: A Guide to the Postclassical World*, edited by G.W. Bowersock, Peter Brown, and Oleg Grabar, 238–57. Cambridge, MA: Belknap Press of Harvard University Press, 1999.

Majercik, Ruth. *The Chaldean Oracles: Text, Translation, and Commentary*. Leiden: E. J. Brill, 1989.

Majercik, Ruth. "Chaldean Triads in Neoplatonic Exegesis: Some Reconsiderations." *Classical Quarterly* 51, no. 1 (2001): 265–96.

Marx-Wolf, Heidi. "High Priests of the Highest God: Third-Century Platonists as Ritual Experts." *Journal of Early Christian Studies* 18, no. 4 (December 22, 2010): 481–513.

Marx-Wolf, Heidi. "Pythagoras the Theurgist: Porphyry and Iamblichus on the Role of Ritual in the Philosophical Life." In *Religious Competition in the Third Century CE: Jews, Christians, and the Greco-Roman World*, edited by Jordan Rosenblum, Lily Vuong, and Nathaniel DesRosiers, 32–38. Göttingen, Germany: Vandenhoeck and Ruprecht, 2014.

Marx-Wolf, Heidi. "Medicine." In *Late Ancient Knowing: Explorations in Intellectual History*, edited by C. M. Chin and Moulie Vidas, 80–98. Berkeley: University of California Press, 2015.

Marx-Wolf, Heidi. *Spiritual Taxonomies and Ritual Authority: Platonists, Priests, and Gnostics in the Third Century C.E.* Philadelphia: University of Pennsylvania Press, 2016.

Marx-Wolf, Heidi. "Living Plants, Dead Animals, and Other Matters: Embryos and Demons in Porphyry of Tyre." *Preternature: Critical and Historical Studies on the Preternatural* 7, no. 1 (March 16, 2018): 1–26.

Morgan, Janett. "Women, Religion, and the Home." In *A Companion to Greek Religion*, edited by Daniel Ogden, 297–310. Malden, MA: Wiley-Blackwell, 2007.

Murphy-Morgan, Sharon Lorraine. "Women and Death Rituals in Late Antiquity: Forming the Christian Identity." Master's Thesis, University of Calgary, 2011.

Nathan, Geoffrey S. *The Family in Late Antiquity: The Rise of Christianity and the Endurance of Tradition.* London: Routledge, 2000.

O'Meara, Dominic. *Pythagoras Revived: Mathematics and Philosophy in Late Antiquity.* Oxford: Oxford University Press, 1991.

Penella, Robert J. *Greek Philosophers and Sophists in the Fourth Century A.D.: Studies in Eunapius of Sardis.* Leeds: Francis Cairns, 1990.

Penniman, John David. "Fed to Perfection: Mother's Milk, Roman Family Values, and the Transformation of the Soul in Gregory of Nyssa." *Church History* 84, no. 3 (2015): 495–530.

Richlin, Amy. *Arguments with Silence: Writing History of Roman Women.* Ann Arbor: University of Michigan Press, 2014.

Rizakis, Athanasios. "Urban Elites in the Roman East: Enhancing Regional Positions and Social Superiority." In *A Companion to Roman Religion*, edited by Jörg Rüpke, 317–30. Malden, MA: Blackwell, 2011.

Rüpke, Jörg. *A Companion to Roman Religion.* Blackwell Companions to the Ancient World: Literature and Culture. Malden, MA: Blackwell, 2011.

Schwaizer, Helmut. "Domestic Architecture in Ephesus from the Hellenistic Period to Late Antiquity." In *Mediterranean Families in Antiquity: Households, Extended Families, and Domestic Space*, edited by Sabine R. Huebner and Geoffrey S Nathan, 79–92. Malden, MA: Wiley-Blackwell, 2017.

Scott, Joan W. "Gender: A Useful Category of Historical Analysis." *American Historical Review* 91, no. 5 (1986): 1053–75.

Shaw, Gregory. *Theurgy and the Soul: The Neoplatonism of Iamblichus.* University Park: Pennsylvania State University Press, 1995.

Shaw, Gregory. "Neoplatonic Theurgy and Dionysius the Areopagite." *Journal of Early Christian Studies* 7, no. 4 (1999): 573–99.

Sherrer, Peter. "The City of Ephesos from the Roman Period to Late Antiquity." In *Ephesos: Metropolis of Asia*, edited by Helmut Koester, 1–25. Cambridge, MA: Harvard University Press, 1995.

Stang, Charles M. *Our Divine Double.* Cambridge, MA: Harvard University Press, 2016.

Stefaniw, Blossom. "Knowledge in Late Antiquity: What Is It Made of and What Does It Make?" *Studies in Late Antiquity* 2, no. 3 (September 1, 2018): 266–93.

Stratton, Kimberly B., and Dayna S. Kalleres, eds. *Daughters of Hecate: Women and Magic in the Ancient World*. Oxford: Oxford University Press, 2014.

Tanaseanu-Döbler, Ilinca. "Religious Education in Late Antique Paganism." In *Religious Education in Pre-Modern Europe*, edited by Ilinca Tanaseanu-Döbler and Marvin Döbler, 97–146. Leiden: Brill, 2012.

Tanaseanu-Döbler, Ilinca. "Sosipatra—Role Models for Pagan 'Divine' Women in Late Antiquity." In *Divine Men and Women in the History and Society of Late Hellenism*, edited by Maria Dzielska and Kamilla Twardowska, 123–47. Krakow, Poland: Jagiellonian University Press, 2013.

Tanaseanu-Döbler, Ilinca. *Theurgy in Late Antiquity: The Invention of a Ritual Tradition*. Göttingen, Germany: Vandenhoeck and Ruprecht, 2013.

Upson-Saia, Kristi. "Gender and Narrative Performance in Early Christian Cross-Dressing Saints' Lives." *Studia Patristica* 45 (2010): 43–48.

Urbano, Arthur P. *The Philosophical Life: Biography and the Crafting of Intellectual Identity in Late Antiquity*. Patristic Monograph Series, vol. 21. Washington, DC: Catholic University of America Press, 2013.

Uždavinys, Algis. *Philosophy and Theurgy in Late Antiquity*. Kettering: Angelico Press, 2010.

Van Der Eijk, Philip J. "Principles and Practices of Compilation and Abbreviation in the Medical 'Encyclopaedias' of Late Antiquity." In *Condensing Text—Condensed Texts*, edited by Marietta Horster and Christiane Reitz, 519–54. Stuttgart: Franz Steiner Verlag, 2010.

Vidal, Gore. *Julian*. Reprint ed. New York: Vintage, 2003.

Vuolanto, Ville. "Elite Children, Socialization, and Agency in the Late Roman World." In *The Oxford Handbook of Childhood and Education in the Classical World*, edited by Judith Evans Grubbs and Tim Parkin, 580–99. Oxford: Oxford University Press, 2013.

Ward, Benedicta. *Harlots of the Desert: A Study of Repentance in Early Monastic Sources*. Kalamazoo, MI: Cistercian, 1978.

Watts, Edward Jay. "Orality and Communal Identity in Eunapius' Lives of the Sophists and Philosophers." *Byzantion*, no. 75 (2005): 334–61.

Watts, Edward Jay. "The Student Self in Late Antiquity." In *Religion and the Self in Antiquity*, edited by David Brakke, Michale L. Satlow, and Steven Weitzman, 234–51. Bloomington: Indiana University Press, 2005.

Watts, Edward Jay. *City and School in Late Antique Athens and Alexandria*. Berkeley: University of California Press, 2006.

Watts, Edward Jay. "Education: Speaking, Thinking and Socializing." In *Oxford Handbook of Late Antiquity*, edited by Scott Fitzgerald Johnson, 467–86. Oxford: Oxford University Press, 2012.

Watts, Edward Jay. *The Final Pagan Generation*. Transformation of the Classical Heritage, 53. Oakland: University of California Press, 2015.

Watts, Edward Jay. *Hypatia: The Life and Legend of an Ancient Philosopher*. Women in Antiquity. New York: Oxford University Press, 2017.

Wendt, Heidi. *At the Temple Gates: The Religion of Freelance Experts in the Roman Empire*. Oxford: Oxford University Press, 2016.

Index

For the benefit of digital users, indexed terms that span two pages (e.g., 52–53) may, on occasion, appear on only one of those pages.

adolescence, 21, 33, 46–48, 49, 69–70

Aedesius, 6–7, 11–12, 14–15, 50, 53, 54, 67, 68, 70–71, 73, 74, 76–77, 78–80, 81, 100–2, 103

Amelius, 76, 95, 104

Ammonius Saccas, 75–76, 87, 91–92, 94–95

ancient biography/ancient biographical writing, 1–3, 8–9, 13, 14–15, 17–19, 43, 92–93, 94, 96–97, 111

angel, 4–6, 36–37, 39–40, 85, 87, 88–89

Antoninus (Sosipatra's son), 7–8, 51–52, 54–55, 67–68, 69–71, 84–85, 111, 112–13

Apollo, 95, 97, 106–7

Apollonius of Tyana, 93, 94–95

apotheosis, 104

Aristotle, 35, 67, 74–75, 80–81

Artemis, 19, 26–27, 49, 61–63

Asia/Asia Minor, 3–4, 9–10, 19, 26–27, 49, 53, 54, 58–59, 60–61, 67, 100–2, 116–17

assimilation (to divinity), 3–4, 9–10, 43, 82–83, 91–93, 98–99, 100–2

astrology, 4–6, 41–42, 57–58, 88–89

astronomy, 57–58

Augustine of Hippo, 17–19, 39, 51, 55–56, 70, 104–5

baths/bathing, 21–22, 26–27, 48, 54, 58, 60–61, 64, 66–67, 77, 97, 98–99, 100

betrothal, 46–47, 49–50, 51, 52–53, 70

bios/bioi, 2–3

breast feeding, 64–65

breast milk, 64–67

Cappadocia, 50–51, 53, 54, 68, 73, 100–2

celestial body/bodies, 85, 88–89

celestial journey, 104–5

celestial realm(s), 85, 96, 104–5

celibacy, 55

Chaldean/Chaldean expert/Chaldean initiate, 4–6, 36–37, 57–58, 73, 76–77, 82–83, 88–89, 104

Chaldean lore/Chaldean wisdom, 4–6, 35, 50, 70–71, 88–89

Chaldean Oracles, 10–11, 36–37, 82–83

chastity, 48, 54–55

childbirth, 17–20, 25, 45, 46–47, 54–55, 59–60, 63–64

childhood/stages of childhood, 3–4, 15, 17–20, 21, 30, 49, 63–64

child mortality rates, 20–21, 45, 63–64

childrearing, 17–19, 24–25, 43, 46–47, 64, 112

Christianity, 55, 110–11, 116–17

Chrysanthius, 1–2, 8–9, 11–12, 33, 78, 102–3, 112

civic cult/civic religion, 26–27, 49, 59, 60–63

Concordia, 45, 55–56

Constantinople, 21–22, 54

cosmic harmony, 41

cosmic sympathy, 11, 41–42

curriculum, 39, 40, 74, 78–79, 80–81, 82–83, 96–97